Otaku

OTAKU

JAPAN'S DATABASE ANIMALS

Hiroki Azuma

Translated by Jonathan E. Abel and Shion Kono

University of Minnesota Press
Minneapolis • London

Originally published in Japanese as *Dōbutsuka suru posutomodan: otaku kara mita nihon shakai* (Tokyo: Kōdansha Gendai Shinsho, 2001). © Hiroki Azuma 2001

English translation copyright 2009 by the Regents of the University of Minnesota

Published by the University of Minnesota Press
111 Third Avenue South, Suite 290
Minneapolis, MN 55401-2520
http://www.upress.umn.edu

Library of Congress Cataloging-in-Publication Data

Azuma, Hiroki, 1971–
    [Dōbutsuka suru posutomodan. English]
    Otaku : Japan's database animals / Hiroki Azuma ; translated by
Jonathan E. Abel and Shion Kono.
        p.   cm.
    Includes bibliographical references and index.
    ISBN 978-0-8166-5351-5 (hc : alk. paper) — ISBN 978-0-8166-5352-2
(pb : alk. paper)
    1. Subculture—Japan.   2. Popular culture—Japan.   3. Japan—
Civilization—1945–   I. Title.
    HN723.5.A9513   2009
    306'.10952—dc22   2008040819

Printed in the United States of America on acid-free paper

The University of Minnesota is an equal-opportunity educator and employer.

23   10 9 8 7 6

CONTENTS

Preface to the English Edition

Hiroki Azuma

I am a Japanese critic who was born in 1971. In my twenties, I contributed articles to literary and critical journals while studying philosophy in graduate school. My first book was a monograph on a French philosopher, but around the same time I published a collection of essays that broadly discussed social issues and subculture—a collection for which I am more widely known in the Japanese mass media. The present work is my fourth book in Japanese.

In this book, I focused on the "otaku"—a subculture that emerged in Japan in the 1970s and gave rise to a massive entertainment industry producing manga, anime, and video games. By understanding its history through the notion of "postmodernity," I wanted to analyze the psychological structure of contemporary Japan. This book was published in Japanese in 2001, and it held particularly strong influence for young readers interested in contemporary society and subculture. This English translation is the third, Korean and French translations having been previously published.

This book discusses Japanese society with a Japanese audience in mind. The forms of otaku culture dealt with in this book have been well received in the United States and Europe, especially among the younger generation. Also, as discussed in chapter 1, otaku culture has both a portion of its origin in American subculture and a background in the worldwide transformation of modern society. Therefore, the project of the book—to explore the psychological structure of the age through a brief history of subcultural products such as manga, anime, and video games—is valid not only in Japan but to a certain extent in the United States and Europe. With the publication of this book, I look forward to receiving unanticipated responses from readers outside Japan.

The Translators' Introduction situates this book in the tradition of Japanese "criticism," citing the names of Karatani Kōjin and Asada Akira. The term "criticism" here requires comment. Since the 1980s, the Japanese word *hihyō* (generally translated as *criticism*) refers not simply to literary criticism but has become a uniquely nuanced piece of jargon. It represents a particular style of scholarship greatly influenced over the past thirty years by new paradigms such as postmodernism, postcolonialism, and cultural studies, and it is probably closest to what "theory" refers to in English. The reflections in this book, it is certainly true, are constructed in close proximity to such paradigms. Therefore, it is completely appropriate to situate this book as a "critical" or "theoretical" work. I feel privileged that my work will be published for the same general audience as the theoretical works that have deeply influenced my own thinking.

However, I wish to point out that, although this book is indeed a work of "criticism" and "theory," it was not necessarily published as such. The Japanese edition of this book was originally published as an inexpensive paperback, available to a wider range of audiences interested in the relationships between contemporary society and subculture. In fact, in terms of reader responses, I received many more responses from general readers than from academics. In this sense, this English edition will be launched in a very different environment from that of the Japanese edition.

This book was not originally published as "criticism" because at that time Japanese "criticism" was at a major turning point. Postmodernism was introduced to Japan in earnest in the 1980s. Karatani and Asada represented the movement and exerted great influence until the early 1990s. By the late 1990s, their role declined rapidly, and, dragged down by this decline, works of "criticism" and "theory" in general began to lose readership. In the face of such a crisis, I wrote this book in order to resuscitate "criticism" and "theory" by treating a completely different subject matter, aiming at a completely different readership from what postmodernists of the past generation had assumed. In Japanese criticism, Ōtsuka Eiji and Miyadai Shinji had been virtually neglected until the publication of this book. Therefore, by discussing the otaku using postmodernist theories and by mentioning Ōtsuka and Miyadai while neglecting Karatani, my account of affairs in this book contained strategic reversals of values that were considered very bold at the time.

The Japanese edition of this book was published not as a simple study of postmodernity, but it was conceived, written, and published as a critical intervention very much cognizant of the Japanese discursive space in the 1990s into the 2000s. Such politics will probably be lost in translation. I do not believe that this loss is bad. In any translation, original contexts will be lost, and this English edition has a different role from that of the Japanese version. I still wish to write about this situation because knowledge of the politics of this book will facilitate not only the understanding of the book itself but also the understanding of the situation in which Japanese criticism and theory in general are placed.

I believe that, as of now, Japanese critical and theoretical discourse can roughly be divided into two groups. On the one hand, just as in English-language theory, various critical works analyze contemporary Japanese society while absorbing the shocks of postmodernism, postcolonialism, cultural studies, sociology, and historical studies. My book belongs in this group, and in the past several years excellent work has continued to appear in this category, written mainly by scholars in their thirties: Morikawa Kaichirō's *Shuto no tanjō* (2003, "The birth of the hobby city," on the emergence of Akihabara as the premier otaku district); Kitada Akihiro's *Warau Nihon no 'nationalism'* (2005, "Snickering of Japanese 'nationalism,'" on Japanese subculture); and Itō Gō's *Tezuka izu Deddo* (2005, "Tezuka is dead," on the manga form after Tezuka Osamu), to name a few that I feel are worthy of English translation. On the other hand, as indicated in the words quoted in the Translators' Introduction, there are still those critics and theorists of an older sort who ignore such trends and continue to talk about "the end of literature" or "the end of criticism." The works by the former are, unfortunately, rarely known outside Japan; those introduced in foreign countries as Japanese critics and theorists are mostly from the latter group.

I have always felt that such an environment has been a huge impediment to communication, both for Japanese writers and scholars and for scholars outside Japan who want to know about Japan today. As the author of this book, it would be my utmost pleasure if its publication becomes an occasion for readers to become interested, beyond this volume, in this "new criticism" in general.

Here I should probably account for the time between the publication of the original Japanese version and this English translation. As discussed in the Translators' Introduction, the sequel to this book has already been published in Japanese. The title of the sequel can be translated as "The Birth of Gamelike Realism." While continuing the analysis of the current situation, it asks the following questions: If the otaku continue to embark on narratives within the "animalistic" world of "database consumption" depicted in the present volume, what does this "will for narrative" mean? Under these conditions, how are work and authorship reconceived? More than half of the longer sequel is devoted to textual analysis of individual works. The objects of interpretation are not regular novels but those works called "light novels" and "beautiful girl games," new forms of narrative created by the Japanese otaku in the first half of the 2000s.

As discussed above, a will for a departure from existing criticism and theory is inscribed in the concept of *Otaku: Japan's Database Animals*. In comparison, "The Birth of Gamelike Realism" is a book that is far more literary and critical in the traditional sense. In the sequel, Karatani's name once again figures prominently and novelist Murakami Haruki appears at the end as well. Instead of emphasizing the paradigm shifts between the world of criticism that gave scant attention to pop culture and this newer mode of critique, I am attempting to prepare a common linguistic base that enables the analysis of both the new literature created by the animalistic otaku and the novels heretofore known as literature. This attempt has been welcomed with good reviews for the most part, but some younger (and otaku) readers have attacked me for being too conservative and boring. At present, I am mired in this sort of controversy in the Japanese-language sphere. And though there is no need for English-language readers to know about such debates, one thing I wish to convey is the speed of these changes and the rise of a new readership attuned to them. The changes are illustrated by my own transitions: while in 2001 I emphasized a break with the critical status quo, by 2007 I found it necessary to be conscious of the continuities. In 2001, it was scandalous to take up the otaku in criticism; in 2007, not appreciating the cutting-edge nature of otaku is considered ample cause for critical reproach.

Between 2001 and 2007, the otaku forms and markets quite rapidly won social recognition in Japan. In 2003, Miyazaki Hayao won the Academy Award for his *Spirited Away*; around the same time Murakami Takashi achieved recognition for otaku-like designs; in 2004, the Japanese pavilion in the 2004 International Architecture Exhibition of Venice Biennale (Biennale Architecture) featured "otaku." In 2005, the word *moe*—one of the keywords of the present volume—was chosen as one of the top ten "buzzwords of the year." Akihabara, a Tokyo district in which the otaku gather, is now one of the most attention-grabbing districts in Japan. And authors who made their debuts with the aforementioned "light novels" and "beautiful girl games" have gone on to write one best seller after another and to win numerous prestigious literary prizes. Through these changes in circumstances, the otaku have changed and so too have the readers and the objects of critical discourse. Otaku forms and markets remained the objects of critical description in the original 2001 publication. In 2007, however, the otaku are the principal readers of the "new critical discourse" in Japan, and their subculture is enveloped and being reconstructed within it. At least for me, subculture for the otaku is no longer the object of analysis but is transforming into the very environment of criticism, in which the power of words is circulated and tested.

I would like to acknowledge and thank some of the people involved in this project. I cannot adequately thank the two translators, Shion Kono and Jonathan Abel. The publication of this book did not follow the usual process, in which an English-language publisher or literary agent contacts the Japanese publisher and then translators are selected. Instead, this translation was made possible as these two translators, who became interested in the content of the book, contacted the author directly, voluntarily completed the translation manuscript, and brought the manuscript to publishers. In other words, they were not only translators but also played the role of my agent. Indeed, the author negotiated with the publisher only through them throughout the editing process.

The movement of "new criticism" in Japan has hardly been introduced to the English-language audience yet. If this book becomes a precursor and introduces a breath of fresh air into the intellectual communication between the English-language audience and Japan, all credits should go to the passion of Mr. Kono and Mr. Abel, who discovered this book early, translated it, and made its publication a reality, when my work is unknown to the English-language audience and departs from the mainstream of Japanese critical tradition. Once again, I thank them truly.

I wish to thank Hiroshi Tanaka, editor at Kōdansha, publisher of the original Japanese edition. I also thank Jason Weidemann, editor at the University of Minnesota Press. I was delighted that the University of Minnesota Press was interested in publishing this book. The Press's humanities books were a mainstay for me when I was a university student, and I am happy that my name will join their line-up of authors.

Finally, I wish to write a small tribute. The translation of this book began with an e-mail message in February 2003 from Minoru Hokari, a historian residing in Australia. Mr. Hokari was a researcher who first suggested that this book be translated into English, and he was working on the translation with Julia Yonetani, his colleague, but he was stricken with a malignant lymphoma and suddenly passed away in May 2004. I met Mr. Hokari only once, but his bright personality and insatiable curiosity impressed me. Even during his fatal battle with illness, Mr. Hokari was concerned about the progress of the translation and he even planned on making a proposal to a publisher during his brief convalescence. I was moved by his sincerity and passion. I regret that I had not met him earlier.

The present translation belongs to Mr. Kono and Mr. Abel, but its starting point was my message from Mr. Hokari. I wish to dedicate this book to him.

—July 21, 2007, from a home overlooking
Ikegami Honmon-ji in Tokyo, Japan

Translators' Introduction

*O*taku: Japan's Database Animals* is a translation of Hiroki
Azuma's 2001 best-selling critical, philosophical, and historical inquiry into contemporary consumer society conducted through a focus on Japanese *otaku* culture. Otaku are those
Japanese, usually males and generally between the ages of 18 and 40,
who fanatically consume, produce, and collect comic books *(manga)*,
animated films *(anime)*, and other products related to these forms of
popular visual culture and who participate in the production and sales
of derivative fan merchandise.[1] Although this subculture began as an
underground network of nerdy social outcasts on the fringe of mainstream commerce, it has become a major economic force: in 2007, the
"otaku market" in Japan is estimated to be a 186.7 billion yen (about
1.7 billion dollar) market.[2] Globally, otaku culture has spawned a large
following and strongly influenced popular culture not only in Japan
but also throughout Asia, the United States, and Europe. *Otaku* explains how this emerging cultural phenomenon has become a focal
point for understanding both Japanese society and the postmodern
world.

Through his examination of otaku as consumers (and producers)
of cultural products, Azuma develops a new understanding of our his-
torically bound sociocultural situation after the rupture and breakdown of modern ideologies. Azuma examines what is left in place of
the absent grand narratives and the effects of this absence on human
behavior. The book proposes a model of the "database animal" as a
new type of consumer in the postmodern information era, arguing

that, rather than reading the stories in a "human" mode of consumption that longs for the existence of and searches for deeper meaning, the cravings of "animalized" otaku are satiated by classifying the characters from such stories according to their traits and anonymously creating databases that catalog, store, and display the results. In turn, the database provides a space where users can search for the traits they desire and find new characters and stories that might appeal to them. Here "database" is not simply the kind of computer program or Web site for storing and retrieving information that humans are finding it increasingly difficult to live without, but rather a model or a metaphor for a worldview, a "grand nonnarrative" that lacks the structures and ideologies ("grand narratives") that used to characterize modern society.

According to Azuma, this compulsion toward "database-ization" is a sign that the postmodern condition animalizes human beings. His use of the term "animalization" derives from Alexandre Kojève's reading of Hegel's *Phenomenology of Spirit* and describes the conditions under which people come to use cultural products for the immediate satisfaction of needs without searching for or desiring profound underlying meaning from them. From a quirky footnote added to the second edition of Kojève's *Introduction to the Reading of Hegel* that describes postwar U.S. culture as animalistic and postwar Japanese culture as snobbish, Azuma extrapolates a reading of the entirety of postwar Japanese society. In Kojève's view of Hegel, the end of history is the end of man, but this "is not a cosmic catastrophe.... not a biological catastrophe either: Man remains alive as animal in *harmony* with Nature."[3] In the footnote expanded for the second edition, the Russian-French philosopher reflects on his recent visits to the United States and Japan through the notion of the end of history. Since so much of the book that follows here is owed to Kojève's placing into relation the posthistorical and the animal, we find it necessary to quote from the footnote at length:

> One can ... say that, from a certain point of view, the United States has already attained the final stage of Marxist "communism," seeing that, practically, all the members of a "classless society" can from now

on appropriate for themselves everything that seems good to them, without thereby working any more than their heart dictates.

Now, several voyages of comparison made (between 1948 and 1958) to the United States and the U.S.S.R. gave me the impression that if the Americans give the appearance of being rich Sino-Soviets, it is because the Russians and Chinese are only Americans who are still poor but are rapidly proceeding to get richer. I was able to conclude from this that the "American way of life" was the type of life specific to the post-historical period, the actual presence of the United States in the World prefiguring the "eternal present" future of all humanity. Thus, Man's return to animality appeared no longer as a possibility that was yet to come, but as a certainty that was already present.

It was following a recent voyage to Japan (1959) that I had a radical change of opinion on this point. There I was able to observe a Society that is one of a kind, because it alone has for almost three centuries experienced life at the "end of History"—that is, in the absence of all civil or external war (following the liquidation of feudalism by the roturier Hideyoshi and the artificial isolation of the country conceived and realized by his noble successor Yiyeasu). Now the existence of the Japanese nobles, who ceased to risk their lives (even in duel) and yet did not for that begin to work, was anything but animal.

"Posthistorical" Japanese civilization undertook ways diametrically opposed to the "American way." No doubt, there were no longer in Japan any Religion, Morals, or Politics in the "European" or "historical" sense of these words. But *Snobbery* in its pure form created disciplines negating the "natural" or "animal.... [I]n spite of persistent economic and political inequalities, all Japanese without exception are currently in a position to live according to totally formalized values— that is values empty of all "human content" in the "historical" sense.[4]

Here Kojève first finds a similarity between the U.S. and Japanese postwar cultures: both are posthistorical, that is, beyond the point of history when prototypical struggles of humanity (wars and revolutions) continue to hold sway over the masses. However, while he labels posthistorical U.S. consumers "animalistic" because of their seeming return to a classless, humanless nature, Kojève finds the Japanese snobbish because of the preeminence of a set of codes that have "nothing to do with the *risk* of life in a [warlike or revolutionary] Fight waged for the sake of 'historical' values that have social or political content."[5] These readings of American and Japanese cultures are both exceedingly rich and not particularly sensitive to the historical realities of the postwar period in either culture.[6] As fundamentally flawed as some of the assumptions Kojève makes regarding the United States and Japan are, there is much to be made by his defining of the field of what is at stake in the sweeping postwar cultural shifts whether or not one chooses to find it efficacious to continue to buy into the Western philosophical conceit of differentiating the qualities of what constitutes the human from other living things or modes of being.[7]

In *Otaku*, Hiroki Azuma provides one of the most sustained reflections on and critiques of this distinction. Drawing on Kojève, Azuma turns the footnote on its head, noting that, with the advent of postwar Americanization, *Japan* became animalized. To be more sensitive to the posthistorical conditions of Japan than Kojève, Azuma further argues that consumption by otaku in the 1990s is marked by the proliferation of simulacra (cultural products that are neither originals nor copies) and the increasing emphasis on fiction (and the weakening of the sense of connection with reality). For Azuma, this new era witnessed a new mode of animalized consumer behavior wherein consumption is driven by satiable cravings rather than human desires that could be neither fulfilled nor quenched. In this sense, Azuma's argument is in part a commentary on the social reality of the post-bubble years in the 1990s,[8] characterized by some cataclysmic events in 1995—the Aum Shinrikyō Tokyo subway sarin gas attack and the Kobe earthquake—and larger social change marked by youth phenomena such as *enjo kōsai* (compensated dating) and *hikikomori* (acute social withdrawal). Still, by discussing otaku culture as a symptom of postmodern society, Azuma reveals how the otaku phenomenon both is and is not a Japanese phenomenon. That is to say, it has some native origins in the unique history of postwar Japan, but it is also a product of the late stage of global capitalism that results from larger world-historical conditions. Rather than sealing off the space in which otaku culture must be considered exotic or uniquely Japanese, as previous studies have done,[9] Azuma's nuanced understanding reveals the otaku phenomenon to have far greater and more profound importance beyond the borders of a fringe subculture in Japan. His work enables comparisons of otaku culture to not only the vast fan cultures present in Japan[10] but also, for instance, Star Trek fanatics (Trekkies or Trekkers) in the United States, Web 2.0 Internet culture including blogs and YouTube, the growth of cults and new religions around the world since the 1970s, and even recent antiglobalism protests. For Azuma, the reading and consuming habits of otaku present one clear case of postmodernity's impact on humanity—we are all becoming animalized.

With content that applies an obscure footnote in a book about a notoriously difficult philosopher to the conditions of a contemporary pop cultural phenomenon, it may come as a surprise to English-speaking, and particularly North American, audiences that the Japanese original version of *Otaku* became a bestseller. Since *Dōbutsuka suru posutomodan: otaku kara mita Nihon shakai* (literally translatable as "Animalizing Postmodernity: Japanese Society Seen through Otaku," published in Tokyo by Kōdansha in 2001) first appeared in Japanese, it has gained wide public attention in Japan. By March 2008, it was in its sixteenth printing, having sold more than 63,000 copies. With the publication of Korean, French, and now English translations of the book, the global reception promises to echo its mass reception in Japan. But exactly how and why, we might ask, did the book become a bestseller and even spawn a sequel?

Although the level of education in Japan, the range of the Japanese publishing industry, and the mass marketing of such books of criticism in Japan each played a role in the book's success,[11] the answer may lie less in these macrophenomena than in Azuma's choice to launch his critique in a journalistic rather than academic idiom. Although this phenomenon may seem strange and even awkward in English letters, the casual style of this book is widespread in the Japanese publishing world, which is not so strictly divided between academic and trade publications.

What makes Azuma's study of otaku culture a critical milestone is his ability to commingle high theory with subculture in an accessible style and readable voice at a historical moment when both postmodern thought and otaku were all the rage. Azuma's journalistic approach also reflects an inherent tension between his two registers of critical inquiry and pop cultural criticism, a tension that was refreshing to many readers but anathema to others. As Azuma explains in his Preface, the original publication of *Otaku* in Japanese in 2001 was consciously intended as a critical intervention into what he perceived at the time to be a Japanese scholarly discourse that had become dysfunctional, continually failing to bridge the gap between the theoretical, scholarly world and the worlds of popular culture. The hybrid style of his prose combines its sober, relaxed, scholarly statements with quick, energetic assertions that may make academics uneasy (the flavor of these we tried to convey truthfully in this translation)[12] and is perhaps both symptomatic of when it was produced and peculiar to the challenge Azuma met in writing this book.

The roots of Azuma's theoretical language have less to do with the ivory towers of the academic establishment than the peculiar conditions of intellectual discourse in contemporary Japan. The crucial advent of a critical movement dubbed as "New Academism" in the early 1980s shaped the contours of mainstream critical discourse. New Academism refers to a group of interdisciplinary scholarly works written for an audience much wider than the narrowly defined scholarly circles and influenced by a wide range of critical and cultural theories, most notably postmodern and poststructuralist thinkers of the West such as Jean Baudrillard, Jean-François Lyotard, Jacques Lacan, and Jacques Derrida. By combining theoretical language with shrewd marketing, these works succeeded in making highly theoretical topics such as postmodernism, Saussurian linguistics, neo-Marxism, and psychoanalytic theory marketable and even fashionable. Beyond the academic understanding of their texts, however, the whole movement was interpreted—by many Japanese readers, if not by the authors themselves—as a lifestyle: breaking with tradition, redefining Japanese culture, and (rather problematically) a wholehearted affirmation of consumerism. The players in this movement—writers, critics, artists, and even advertising copywriters, often called the "New Homo Sapiens" *(shinjinrui)*—were followed as celebrities and enthusiastically supported by younger generations. This personality-driven discursive culture has historical roots in the culture of the literati or *bundan* since the Meiji period, but in the early 1980s it entered into another phase with the highly sophisticated consumer culture of the post-high-growth Japan in the background. Asada Akira (b. 1957) exemplifies the New Academism. His *Structure and Power,* a schematic but hardly accessible introduction to poststructuralist thought (in particular Lacanian psychoanalysis), sold more than 100,000 copies, and the *schizo* and the *parano*—terms from one of his books for the schizophrenic and the paranoiac—were chosen as "buzzwords of the year" in 1984.[13] Asada, a young academic with a pale face, became a media darling and it became a vogue for young adults to carry around a copy of *Structure and Power.*[14] Although the initial boom waned in the ensuing years, the movement influenced many young readers, infusing theoretical language into the popular idiom, and catapulted those intellectuals outside of academia but well versed in such language to the forefront of critical discourse.

The success of New Academism in the previous decade paved the way for Azuma's quick ascent to critical stardom. In 1993, roughly a decade after the height of the New Academism fever, Azuma made his critical debut in the journal *Hihyō kūkan* (Critical space), the journal founded and coedited by Asada and another major literary critic of the era, Karatani Kōjin (b. 1941).[15] His debut as a twenty-one-year-old undergraduate at the University of Tokyo drew comparisons with Asada's. His 1998 critical study of Jacques Derrida's later works, *Son-zaironteki, yūbinteki* (Ontological, postal), was serialized originally in *Hihyō kūkan.* Engaging with developments in deconstruction and cultural studies, the book ties together Japanese and Western developments in deconstructive theory that, as a synthetic and original thematic reading of Derrida, is rivaled only by Rodolphe Gasché's *The Tain of the Mirror.* For this work, Azuma won the Suntory Prize for Social Sciences and Humanities and was widely recognized as a provocative thinker with a deep concern for philosophical inquiry as a means to realize social change rather than as an end unto itself.

Azuma was introduced to the critical scene as Asada Akira's successor, someone who would carry postmodern critical discourse as defined by Asada and Karatani into the next generation; however, Azuma's avid interest in otaku culture was met with ambivalence in Asada's circle. With the following words, Asada Akira introduced Azuma in 1998 to world of Japanese letters as the new bright young star at *Hihyō kūkan*:

> The encounter with Hiroki Azuma was a fresh surprise. Of course, the "postmodern intellectuals" of my generation have shown interest in subculture, but it was often just a gesture to break down the barriers between high culture and subculture and without devoting genuine passion for subculture. But here is a bona fide "otaku"—he, in his mid-twenties, still has anime posters in his room and grows a beard imitating an anime director—who is born into thorough cultural poverty after high culture has been completely devastated but nonetheless struggles tenaciously with the French texts (though he cannot speak French himself) and writes papers that make readers think seriously. It was a surprise, after all, and with that surprise, I had to admit that my *Structure and Power* has finally become a thing of the past. Azuma's future success will prove that his "otaku philosophy" *[otaku tetsugaku]* is not at all the same thing as an "otaku *of* philosophy" *[tetsugaku otaku]*.[16] (Translators' emphasis added.)

On the one hand, according to Asada, Azuma embodies something that was never seen: the "genuine passion for subculture." Moreover, Azuma was not to be "an otaku of philosophy"—someone who obsessively accumulates trivia of philosophy without engaging with the ideas or thinking critically about them—but an "otaku philosopher"—someone who theorizes the emerging subculture not just as a subculture but as the subject of serious intellectual discussion for the higher purpose of finding hitherto hidden meaning or as a means for social change and even as indicative of the larger patterns of late capitalism. But this introduction by Asada already shows signs that the forum provided by *Hihyō kūkan* would be ultimately too limiting for Azuma. Significantly, when the above quotation was excerpted for use as an advertisement for *Sonzaironteki, yūbinteki*, Asada's references to otaku and otaku culture had been left out; the blurb on the jacket read simply: "The encounter with Hiroki Azuma was a fresh surprise. . . . with that surprise, I had to admit that my *Structure and Power* has finally become a thing of the past." While the New Academism can be placed in wider social contexts of the 1980s high-consumerist Japan, its practitioners tended to limit their subject matter to the realm of high culture: Western philosophy, classical music, architecture, avant-garde art. Although the otaku subculture since then has belatedly been noticed first by mainstream culture and at last by intellectuals, the strategic deletions of this advertisement here underscore the perception that it was something Asada would regard only as the product of "a thorough cultural poverty after high culture has been completely devastated" and that its traces should be effaced from the "serious" theoretical forum.[17]

In *Otaku*, however, Azuma attempts to cast light on the critical blind spot: to talk about otaku culture in the theoretical language prepared by the New Academism.[18] Responding to a group of critics who read otaku in isolation from wider global and historical concerns, Azuma draws on a range of well-known concepts from Western postmodernist theorists, such as Jean-François Lyotard's analysis of the decline of grand narratives and their replacement with *petits récits,* Jean Baudrillard's concept of the rise of the simulacra, and Gilles Deleuze and Félix Guattari's notion of the rhizome. In addition, Azuma draws on the growing body of criticism by younger critics on Japanese subculture in general, rather than the criticism on specifically otaku culture that was beginning to emerge even then.[19] Particularly influential to him was Ōtsuka Eiji's (b. 1956) *Monogatari shōhiron* (Theory of narrative consumption), a series of works by Miyadai Shinji (b. 1959) on *kogal* (high school girls deeply immersed in the urban culture), and Ōsawa Masachi's (b. 1958) sociological reflections on new communication technologies and Aum Shinrikyō (the cult responsible for the 1995 sarin gas attack).[20] These critics, some of them sociologists by training, stay close to their subject matter often by employing fieldwork and journalistic narrative style, and (with the exception of Ōsawa) do not write from within the critical forum set up by Asada and Karatani. Azuma's discussion is rooted in the everyday reality of the 1990s Japan described by these writers, and Azuma is informed by key concepts such as Ōtsuka's "narrative consumption" and Ōsawa's "fictional age" (in this edition, the detailed contexts of these additional works are supplied in footnotes). Building upon these concepts, Azuma introduces "database consumption" and "the animal age" as key concepts for his theoretical models, giving much-needed theoretical clarity to the discussion of Japanese popular culture. *Otaku*, then, is the fruit of his fertile and rare ability to write for two often irreconcilable audiences: readers of manga and readers of postmodern theory. In other words, this book translates otaku sensibilities into the register of postmodern theory.[21] Like all translations, the text translated here teeters between differing cultures, threatening to smooth out differences and inject foreign ripples into the placid, domestic ordinary. This shift between the languages of high theory and of low, sub-, pop, or mass culture gives the book its energy and tension.

Azuma's project was not received favorably by Asada and Karatani. Even prior to the book's publication, Asada scoffed at Azuma's plan as a kind of neo-nativist return to Japaneseness—"J-turn" *(J-kaiki)*.[22] Karatani would even view this rise of animalization as the end of literature and lament the demise of the literary. Outside of this critical reception, however, initial reviews suggest that Azuma's critical intervention had the intended effect of preparing a ground for further discussion of otaku culture using the language of critical theory.[23] More importantly, as the commercial success of this book suggests, Azuma succeeded in bringing in a new audience for his scholarly discourse, many of them otaku themselves, sparking ensuing debates at all levels, in print and online. Azuma's prolific critical activities since 2001 include forays not only into various facets of otaku culture and postmodernity but also into a discussion on the issue of freedom and ethics in the information society.[24] Azuma also experiments with a wide range of new media and public forums such as blogs and Internet-driven public colloquia, moving at a frenetic (and some might say reckless) speed. In the process, Azuma became perhaps one of the most visible and controversial Japanese critics in the first decade of the twenty-first century.

Karatani offered a solely negative assessment of the state of post-bubble Japanese cultural production in a 2004 interview titled "The End without Irony" in his book *Kindai bungaku no owari* (The end of modern literature):

Modern literature is over. The traditional culture of intellectuals is over. We can see this phenomenon everywhere. In Europe, anime and manga are trendy....

I don't care in the least that (Japanese) manga and anime are (globally) trendy. If that is Japanese culture, then I guess we could say the whole world is being "Japanized."

However, in reality, the world is not becoming particularly "Japanized." In Japan, intellectual and ethical factors have become extinct. Those who scorn this reign supreme. In the past, when people said that subcultures are good, manga are good, or anime are great, they said it with irony. And to that extent we maintained our critical stance for a time. However, in Japan today there is no longer any irony. There is simply the affirmation of acting like a big fish in a little sea. To put it simply, in today's Japan there is nothing. And so no margin for recovery. Nevertheless, I have not given up hope. From now on, I will continue to work persistently.[25]

Where Karatani and Asada largely avoided criticism of the new cultural forms and modes of consumption in part because they have been reluctant to admit the potential radicality of these new phenomena, Azuma charges ahead—and his radical break and difference from Karatani and his other influences is that he posits a moment or place for that radical change in the otaku world itself. But beyond the resistance for discussing the "low" otaku culture in the language of high theory, there is a substantive difference between Karatani's negative assessment and Azuma's rather optimistic outlook. Like Karatani, Azuma continues to hope for the possibilities of change. Although he recognizes that the situation is in fact bleak (people are being animalized after all), Azuma believes he is doing something about it. He is deeply concerned with the issue of freedom and has even embarked on a kind of cultural activism in recent years, working with academics and manga producers to found a new magazine dedicated to a new form hailed as "light novels" (a central topic in Azuma's *Gēmu teki riarizumu no tanjō: Dōbutsuka suru posutomodan 2* [A birth of gamelike realism: Animalizing postmodernity 2], the 2007 sequel to *Otaku*[26]), and publishing online newsletters with young writers, critics, and otaku fans themselves.

Azuma's detractors have made claims that he is too close to the escapist otaku world to have proper perspective, a critical stance, or a deeper concern for freedom. Whether his goals are attainable or not, Azuma's commitment to them is evident throughout his work. His epilogue to Karatani's collection of essays *Hyūmoa to shite no yuibutsuron* (Materialism as humor) is as much about Karatani as it is about Azuma himself. Azuma writes that humor in Karatani's essay and book is "nothing more than another name for that hope" for a cure to the sicknesses of modernity that Karatani spent the early part of his career defining.[27] In other words, although we might have thought Karatani had turned to a different and more lighthearted subject when he examined humor, in fact nothing had changed; both before and after any supposed ethical or philosophical turn, Karatani was writing about the same thing, though the materials on which he focused his inquiry may have differed. Azuma cautions us not to underestimate the radical importance of humor in Karatani. Azuma's comment on Karatani is instructive for understanding how otaku culture, however animalized, might contain a radical point of transcendence. Here, in this caution not to take Karatani's examination of humor as a whimsical shift from critical theory, we can interpolate a comment on Azuma's own transfer of focus from Derrida to the world of otaku (often considered whimsical and escapist). The shift from one field of inquiry to another is not a shift outside the ethical necessities for criticism outlined in Azuma's early work but rather a deepening of their import through engagement with new content (pop culture). So as with Azuma's reading of continuity in Karatani's career, we should resist the notion of a turn in Azuma's writing from the lofty aims of high theory to the easily commodified work of pop cultural studies—resist reading the moment as a shift from political action through critique to complicit work about a popular subject.

Otaku: Japan's Database Animals is a book that pushes its readers in at least two ways—nowhere more so than in its use of the titular term *animals*. It is in Azuma's use of the animetaphor (a translation par excellence) that the double work of his criticism is most apparent. Western philosophy has repeatedly denied animals access to language, and yet philosophy returns again and again to the scene of the animal cry to delineate the concept of mankind. Whether Aristotle's dog, Heidegger's lizard, or Wittgenstein's lion, animals have been represented as lacking in those things that make us human—language, knowledge, awareness, and imagination. *Otaku* considers the new breed of consumer as lacking the capacity to long for or even express concern for deep, inner meanings—in this sense otaku are without language as it has been hitherto known; they have become animalized. Certainly some readers will find a serious pessimism in Azuma's prediction of the future of humanity—namely the continued animalization of human beings. However, Azuma also emphasizes the need to grasp and confront the present situation. To this extent, his work is vital in that it forces us to engage directly with the supposed depoliticization that has been said to accompany the postmodern condition. Only by grappling with various critiques that consider the position of otaku to be one of apolitical inaction can the possibility of an alternative politics be nurtured. Azuma's argument translates otaku into philosophical terms primarily through his use of animal metaphorics.[28] Using the notion of animetaphor, Akira Mizuta Lippit has written of the (lack of) place of the concept of the animal in Western philosophy:

> the animal figure raises questions about the origin of the metaphor, its place in the world of language. One might posit provisionally that the animal functions not only as an exemplary metaphor but, within the scope of rhetorical language, as an originary metaphor. One finds a fantastic transversality at work between the animal and the metaphor— the animal is already a metaphor, the metaphor an animal. Together they transport to language, the vitality of another life, another expression: animal and metaphor, a metaphor made flesh, a living metaphor that is by definition not a metaphor, antimetaphor—"animetaphor."[29]

So when Azuma calls on Kojève's notion of animality, he invokes an entire tradition of thought on the animal that shows the concept to lack all that is thought essential to the category of human. In so doing, in translating the low culture of otaku into the high domain of criticism with the term "animalize," Azuma risks alienating and making enemies of both the otaku of whom he speaks and the postmodern critics with whom he had been in dialogue since the beginning of his career. On the one hand, he calls otaku "animalistic," and this necessarily (though, as we shall see, not solely) has a negational connotation—that is to say, otaku are not "human" in the enlightenment conception of the human. On the other hand, he pays attention to otaku culture as the essence of the postmodern moment, despite the tendency of much Japanese postmodern criticism of the time to remain snobbishly centered on high culture or at least on cultural forms from the modern period. With this translation, some Americans, who take issue with Kojève's notion of an animalistic America, similarly might be taken aback by the implication of the argument: as Japanese consumer culture became more Americanized after the war, it became more animalized. Kojève and Azuma both figure American-style capitalism as the harbinger of the posthistorical animality. For Azuma this is merely perfected in the modes of otaku production and consumerism.

What Azuma does first and foremost is provide a critique of otaku culture that calls their behavior animalized; theirs is a culture lacking not only a grand narrative but also the power to speak or articulate meaning beyond surfaces. At a deeper level—where, to use Azuma's own terminology, the characteristics of the argument in *Otaku* might be filed away as part of a larger database of "postmodern theories" that would include the categorized terminology and jargon of Lyotard, Baudrillard, and Asada Akira—Azuma's work can be seen as calling into question the very notion of an animal/human distinction in postmodernity. Aren't we all otaku? Aren't we all animalized? Is there nothing else other than to be animalized in this moment? Through this kind of negative dialectics, Azuma inverts an entire line of Western thought on animality. Yes, animals are lacking, but we are all animals. So what? As animals, what can we do? What do animals offer that the human and snobbish alternatives deny?

The translators would first and foremost like to thank Hiroki Azuma for giving us the inspiration and permission to translate his book. We also thank Julia Yonetani and the executrix of the estate of Minoru Hokari for the kind permission to use their translation of chapter 1 as the basis for our retranslation of the chapter; Thomas LaMarre for his introduction to Jason Weidemann at the University of Minnesota Press and for his advice throughout. Greg Pflugfelder and Yurika Kurakata of the Donald Keene Center and Betty Borden and Ryohei Yamamoto of the Japan Society were instrumental in orchestrating Azuma's visit to Columbia University in 2005—a visit that made possible this translation. Madge Huntington at Columbia University was particularly helpful in making suggestions about the initial book proposal. We would also like to thank our two anonymous readers who generously released their names to us and provided more feedback and suggestions as our draft progressed to its current form.

Jonathan Abel thanks his wife, Jessamyn, for her patience throughout the process and kind reading of the manuscript in the final stages. Shion Kono wishes to thank Ryo, his wife, for her rock-solid moral support.

This translation is dedicated to our students, whose keen interest in otaku-related matters prompted us to embark on the project. We hope the volume will be of use as an introduction to students interested in otaku studies who have yet to encounter critical theory and to students of critical theory who have yet to consider otaku studies as a symptom of the contemporary condition. This translation is also dedicated to Minoru Hokari, whom we never met but whose generous spirit lives here.

Otaku

1. The Otaku's Pseudo-Japan

What Is Otaku Culture?

The Figure of the Postmodern as Manifest in the Structure of Otaku Culture

I suppose that everyone has heard of "otaku." Simply put, it is a general term referring to those who indulge in forms of subculture strongly linked to anime, video games, computers, science fiction, special-effects films, anime figurines, and so on. In this book, I identify this form of subculture as "otaku culture."

Otaku culture, as exemplified through comics and anime, still often maintains an image as a youth culture. However, the generation of Japanese people born between the late 1950s and the early 1960s—thirty- and forty-year-olds holding positions of responsibility within society—are actually its core consumers. They are no longer youths enjoying a period of post-college limbo and freedom before taking on social responsibility. In this sense, otaku culture already has some deep roots in Japanese society.

Furthermore, although otaku culture has not expanded nationally to the same extent as has "J-pop"[1] for instance, it is far from insignificant. Estimated from the number of specialist magazines, the size of the fanzine market, and the number of Web sites registered on Internet search engines, the number of consumers of otaku culture is at least several hundred thousand. And that's just counting those active otaku consumers who buy and sell derivative works or take part in cosplay, that is, dressing up in costumes to resemble characters from manga and anime.[2] In addition, the phenomenon of otaku culture is not limited to Japan. As is frequently reported in the mainstream press, the unique world that otaku have produced through comics, anime, video games, and the like has had great impact on subcultures in Korea, Taiwan, and across Asia.

Moreover, from the early 1980s—when closed online communities were the only form of computerized correspondence available— to the present, the foundation of Japan's Internet culture has been formed by the otaku. Their imprint can be seen both up front and behind the scenes, not only in the large number of otaku Web sites and chat rooms but through providers who name FTP sites after anime characters and in the manuals of word-processing and spreadsheet software, where passages from "novel games" (computerized choose-your-own-adventure graphic novels),[3] casually appear as sample sentences in example diagrams.

At this juncture, therefore, any attempt to consider seriously the contemporary conditions of Japanese culture must include an investigation of otaku culture. However, ever since 1988–89, when Miyazaki Tsutomu carried out the kidnapping, rape, and murder of several young girls, the term "otaku" had been burdened with a particularly negative connotation.[4]

Originally "otaku" was used to refer to the supporters of a new subculture that emerged in the 1970s.[5] Unfortunately the term became widely known in connection with this grotesque incident, and as a result otaku in Japan were largely associated with those with antisocial and perverted personality traits. Right after Miyazaki's arrest, one weekly magazine described otaku as those "without basic human communication skills who often withdraw into their own world."[6] This remains the general perception.

On the other hand, a completely opposite position also exists. It is not widely known that, since the 1990s, a certain generation of otaku have come to use the term in a highly positive light. The severe otaku-bashing in the press in the wake of the Miyazaki incident incited a reverse reaction from otaku themselves, who have now become hyperconscious of their identity as otaku. Initially such pretensions largely passed unnoticed by the mass media. However, once *Neon Genesis*

Evangelion (*Shin seiki evangelion,* Anno Hideaki, 1995) became a hit in 1995 and otaku culture gained wide attention, these issues gradually surfaced. One example was the publication of *An Introduction to Otaku Studies (Otakugaku nyūmon)* by cultural critic Okada Toshio[7] in 1996. In his introduction, Okada called into question the way in which "otaku" had become a derogatory term and presented a redefinition of otaku as "those who possessed an evolved vision"—a "new type" of person responsive to the cultural conditions of a highly consumerist society.[8] This almost megalomaniacal claim paradoxically reveals the extent to which otaku feared being typecast.

The divide that formed out of the Miyazaki incident made it difficult to speak objectively and candidly about otaku culture until the end of the 1990s. On the one hand, voices of authority within the mass media and pubic discourse still hold a strong loathing for otaku behavior, and the debate on otaku culture often faces resistance at that level, preempting any meaningful discussion. In fact, I myself was shocked at the fierce opposition I received from a very well-known critic after divulging plans to write this book on anime.[9]

On the other hand, otaku, who usually display an air of anti-authoritarianism, distrust any method that is not otaku-like and do not welcome discussion on anime and video games initiated by anyone other than an otaku. As someone who made his debut on the public stage through an academic journal on contemporary criticism far from the world of subculture, I too have faced opposition from a number of otaku.[10] In other words, some people refuse to even recognize otaku, while others believe only a designated group possesses the right to speak about them. It has been extremely difficult to take a position that does not adhere to either of these stances.

Enabling a critical analysis appropriate to its material, this book attempts to remedy this dysfunctionality with a breath of fresh air so that one can simply say what one means about otaku culture and, in turn, about the current condition of Japanese culture in general. This, finally, should lead to a greater understanding of our society. Just as literature and art have a history, so too does otaku culture (albeit a brief period of only forty years), and this history is certainly a reflection of transformations in Japanese society. No doubt it is also possible to trace this past in a vertical line from start to finish, as the "History of Subculture." But I am interested, rather, in viewing a *cross section* of this history, pulling out the relations between transformations in otaku culture and changes experienced in the rest of society. Through this process, I hope to reflect seriously on the society in which we live—one that contains curious subcultures like the otaku culture. The following discussion is thus directed not only toward otaku who are of my generation and share the same knowledge but also toward the large readership who have never thought, or even had the desire to think, about all things otaku. For these readers, I wish to offer my thesis—that the essence of our era (postmodernity) is extremely well disclosed in the structure of otaku culture—merely as a tool for them to come to terms with the world and comprehend it from their respective positions. If I can accomplish this for as many readers as possible, I would be more than pleased.

The Three Generations of Otaku

Here I would like to briefly explain my reason for employing the somewhat ambiguous term "otaku culture." Due to the complex situation noted above, in the 1990s lengthy discussions were carried out among otaku concerning such issues as "What are otaku?" "What is otaku-like?" "Who is an otaku, and who is not?" However, speaking from my own experience, it is impossible to reach a conclusion on such issues, and, even when tackled, they merely lead to an emotional exchange over each person's identity.[11]

To continue nevertheless, the following two things can be said about that which falls under this vague term "otaku culture": first, the origin of otaku subcultures basically lies in the 1960s; second, there are three different generations of those who embrace otaku culture.[12] These three generations can be divided in the following way.

The first generation centers on those who were born around 1960 and saw *Space Battleship Yamato* (*Uchūsenkan Yamato*, Matsumoto Reiji, 1974) and *Mobile Suit Gundam* (*Kidō senshi Gandamu*, Tomino Yoshi-yuki, 1979) during their teen years. The second generation is made up of those who were born around 1970 and, during their teens, enjoyed the diversified and matured otaku culture produced by the preceding generation. The third generation consists of those who were born around 1980 and were junior high school students at the time of the *Neon Genesis Evangelion* boom. The interests of each of these groups differ slightly.

For instance, though the passion for comic, anime, and computers reaches across generations, the first generation's interest in science fiction and B-grade movies has been replaced in the third generation by a thorough fascination with mysteries and computer games. Furthermore, third-generation otaku experienced the spread of the Internet during their teens, and, as a result, their main forum for general fan activities has moved to Web sites, and their interest in illustrations, to computer graphics. Both distribution routes and forms of expression greatly differ from those of earlier generations.[13] The discussion in this book is structured to focus mainly on new trends within the third and most recent of these generations.[14]

The Otaku's Pseudo-Japan

What Is Postmodernity?

I wrote that the essence of *postmodernity* is extremely well disclosed in the structure of otaku culture. And I suppose that many readers have heard of the term "postmodern" somewhere. Given that "post" refers to "after," the literal meaning of "postmodern" is "that which comes after modernity." As such, the fields of contemporary intellectual thought and cultural studies frequently use the concept to broadly describe the cultural world since the 1960s or 1970s.

Thirty to forty years ago, the fundamental conditions that determined the constituents of culture changed within late-capitalist societies of Japan, Europe, and America. Consequently, this change was accompanied by transformations in many areas of cultural production. For example, rock music, special-effects movies, and pop art emerged; LSD and computers were born; politics and literature lost their luster; and the notion of the avant-garde disappeared. Our society is situated in the aftermath of this massive rupture; thus, the current cultural conditions cannot simply be positioned as direct offshoots from fifty or one hundred years ago. For example, the current state of popular entertainment novels, dominated by the genres of mystery, fantasy, and horror, cannot be understood as the direct offshoot of modern Japanese literature. Not only experts in the field, but anyone who has even half seriously come into contact with contemporary culture can grasp, I think, a sense of this rupture. Within the fields of contemporary critical thought, this broadly held intuitive sense of rupture is referred to as "postmodernity."

The term "postmodern" will be used repeatedly throughout this work. However, due to limitations of space I have refrained from conducting a lengthy explanation of the term. I leave the definition of postmodernity to the numerous introductory books on the subject and hope, moreover, that those interested may refer to a theoretical piece about postmodernity on which I am currently working.[15] Of course, I will incorporate an explanation of the concepts to the extent necessary for the following discussion to flow without referring back to such texts. Here I ask merely that you briefly note that when I refer to postmodernity, I am speaking of the period since the 1960s or 1970s, or in terms of Japanese history, the period marked by the era following the Osaka International Expo in 1970—in other words, "the cultural world since the 1970s."

Based on this premise, I will develop the discussion below by focusing on the relation between otaku culture and postmodernity and by presenting various examples. However, prior to that, I must raise one issue in order to comprehend the essence of otaku culture. That is, the relationship between otaku and Japan.

Japanese Images in Otaku Culture

The unique characteristics of otaku culture have often been discussed in comparison with traditional Japanese culture. For example, in his *Theory of Narrative Consumption (Monogatari shōhiron),* published in 1989, the cultural critic Ōtsuka Eiji[16] analyzes the significance of derivative works by drawing on concepts found in kabuki and old-school *bunraku* puppet theater, where each work adheres to a determined

"world" and "idea."[17] Okada also implicitly incorporates this argument
into his previously cited *Introduction to Otaku Studies,* in which he asserts that, in placing the importance of a piece of work on its "idea"
above its message, otaku sensibilities are directly linked to *iki* or the
"urbanity" of Edo culture.[18] The final chapter of Okada's book is titled
"Otaku Are the True Heirs of Japanese Culture."

These claims have been made, for the most part, through a focus
on the consumption patterns of otaku. Yet even in regard to content,
the connection between otaku culture and traditional Japanese culture
has been pointed out frequently. Perhaps the most famous example
comes from contemporary artist Murakami Takashi. According to
Murakami, the unique compositions of animator Kaneda Yoshinori
correspond to the "eccentricities" of Edo painters Kanō Sansetsu and
Soga Shōhaku, while the development of animation figurine making
in the 1990s through the pioneering of figurine makers Bomé and
Tani Akira repeats the history of Buddhist sculptures in Japan.[19]

Even putting aside the arguments of such commentators, one can
easily pick out the sense of compatibility with Japanese images contained within otaku works. For example, Takahashi Rumiko's comic
Urusei Yatsura, which earned a cult following in the early 1980s, became well known for its creation of a unique hybrid world of science
fiction, fantasy, and folklore. This slapstick comedy, in which aliens or
strange beings created from legendary motifs such as ogres, snow-spirits,
and *benzaiten* (a Japanese version of the Hindu goddess of fortune)
appear one after the other dressed in sexually suggestive costumes,
clearly reveals how the otaku fantasy is steeped in Japanese conceits.

This affection for Japanese images continues even now—when
Japanese anime, video, and computer games are being consumed worldwide—to broadly determine otaku culture in a profound way. Or
rather, it could be said that this very affection is now considered a
necessary condition for being an otaku.

For example, the television anime *Martian Successor Nadesico* (*Kidō
senkan Nadeshiko,* Satō Tatsuo, 1996) is a superb work that purpose-
fully puts into perspective this sort of intricate relationship between
the otaku culture and Japanese images while employing metafictional

tricks. The central character of this work is an anime otaku and, at the same time, a fighter who rides on an action robot. These two settings are joined in a circular story of self-fulfillment, as the main character, who dreams of becoming a robot-like anime hero, himself becomes the heroic rider of a robot, just like in a real anime. However halfway through the story, it becomes clear that the main character's "enemy" is, in fact, the military state composed solely of Japanese who employ robot anime as the central tenet of their National Creed. Thus, in the second half of the story he ends up denouncing his former otaku self and fighting the military state that otaku have inadvertently produced. Through parody, this work divulges both the right-wing spirit that robot and action-hero anime of the 1970s possessed as well as the condition of otaku who are unable to find a purpose in life except as mediated through such anime.

In this way, otaku culture is connected in various ways to the problems of Japan. Otaku works often take Japan as the subject matter, use numerous Japanese expressions, and are consumed in a thoroughly Japanese fashion. That otaku culture, for better or for worse, is a subculture unique to Japan has thus been repeatedly emphasized in the existing literature.

However, in actuality the impact of otaku culture now reaches far beyond Japan. As stacks of the translated version of *Card Captor Sakura* (*Kādo kyaputā sakura*, Asaka Morio, 2000) are displayed in Paris bookstores and modified Ayanami Rei figures made in Hong Kong are listed for a hefty prices at Internet auction, today the claim that otaku-like sensibilities are unique to Japan no longer holds such force.[20] As an attempt to understand the development of otaku culture not only within the confines of Japan's national history but also as part of a worldwide postmodernization trend, the plan for this book arose from the recognition of these very conditions. I absolutely do not perceive the emergence of otaku culture as a uniquely Japanese phenomenon. Rather, I think that it should be grasped as one manifestation in Japan of a grand trend toward the postmodernization of culture that began in the middle of the twentieth century. It is precisely for this reason that otakus' works transcend national borders to be well received around the world.

The Source of Otaku Culture Is the United States

But if the rise of otaku culture is part of a global trend, then why have the otaku, as we have seen, come to be fixated on "Japanese things"? Here we have to remind ourselves that, whether it be anime, special-effects films, science fiction films, computer games, or the magazine culture that supports all of these, otaku culture in reality originated as a subculture imported from the United States after World War II, from the 1950s to the 1970s.[21] The history of otaku culture is one of adaptation—of how to "domesticate" American culture. This process also perfectly epitomizes the ideology of Japan during the period of high economic growth. Therefore, if at this time we perceive a Japanese aesthetic in the composition of anime and special effects, it is also necessary to recall that neither anime nor special effects existed in Japan prior to a few decades ago and that their process of becoming "Japanese" is rather convoluted. Otaku may very well be heirs to Edo culture, but the two are by no means connected by a continuous line. Between the otaku and Japan lies the United States.

The process through which "limited animation" was domesticated in Japan illustrates this distortion well. "Limited animation," a term employed in contrast to "full animation," refers to animation made at a rate of eight drawings per second (with three frames of film used per drawing). This method originally emerged in the United States in the late forties in reaction to the realism of Disney animation. Originally, in other words, artists consciously chose this technique in order to draw out the possibilities of animation as a medium of expression. However, in Japan, after the making of *Astroboy* by Tezuka Osamu, this technique was adopted as a necessary evil to make the production of television anime more cost-efficient. In comparison to movies shown at cinemas, television anime had to be made on a low budget and within a short time frame. To decrease the number of drawings per anime, animators relied not only on the "three frames per drawing" technique but also on other methods, such as recycling cells, storing cell pictures in a "bank system," and reusing the same cell with only minor alterations of a character's lips to portray talking. Naturally these limitations dramatically reduced the quality of Japanese anime in comparison to works made in the United States in the 1930s. Critics disparaged this situation, and a classic guide to anime denounced it as early as 1966.[22] It is also well known that Tezuka himself was always dissatisfied with this production environment.

The Unique Aesthetic Developed by Japanese Anime

Yet what is interesting here is the fact that in the 1970s the Japanese anime industry took on their poverty as a positive attribute and conversely developed a unique aesthetic. Animators in the 1970s have been divided broadly into two types: expressionist and narrativist.[23] The former, including animators such as Ōtsuka Yasuo, Miyazaki Hayao, and Takahata Isao, who all began their careers at Toei Animation, essentially preferred full animation techniques and were captivated by the aesthetics of movement. While Miyazaki and Takahata did not fully realize this ideal until the second half of the 1980s, it can already be discerned in their early work, such as Takahata's 1968 production *The Adventures of Hols, Prince of the Sun (Taiyō no ōji: Horusu no daibōken)*. In a manner of speaking, these animators had leanings towards orthodox animation films that conformed to the traditions of Disney and the Fleischer Brothers.

On the other hand, there were also animators such as Rintarō, Yasuhiko Yoshikazu, Tomino Yoshiyuki, and the previously mentioned Kaneda Yoshinori who sought to develop artistic appeal in a different direction from the aesthetics of movement, by working within the confines of limited animation, cell recycling, and the "bank system." Specifically, this led to the enhancement of the worldview and narratives produced in *Space Battleship Yamato, Mobile Suit Gundam,* and *Harmagedon (Genma taisen,* Rintarō, 1983); the refinement of illustrations pioneered by Yasuhiko and Studio Nue; and the unique production rhythm and composition (the still-picture aesthetic) of Kaneda Yoshinori. It was precisely this latter direction that brought Japanese anime to the heart of otaku culture in the 1980s and sprouted a genre with a unique aesthetic far removed from the "animated films" made in the United States.

In short, most of the characteristics of anime since the 1980s that are seen as "otaku-like" or "Japanese" were in fact produced through the mutation of techniques imported from the United States and a positive reappraisal of the results. The emergence of the otaku images of Japan in this way was sustained by the desire to overturn the over-whelmingly inferior status of postwar Japan with respect to the United States and lay claim to this inferior status as itself the embodiment of superiority. Together with the urge toward smaller and more compact radios, cars, and cameras, this process clearly exemplifies the national zeal of the high-economic-growth period. This same desire moreover also appears as a common trait in the works of those writers who highly value otaku culture, such as Okada, Ōtsuka, and Murakami.

By interpreting otakus' favorite Japanese images in this way, we can see that, behind the aforementioned controversy surrounding the assessment of otaku culture, there is a deep-seated collective psychol-ogy beyond the fallout of the Miyazaki incident. Regardless of whether we consider the still-picture aesthetics, the flood of fan works high-lighted by Ōtsuka or the folklore-like world of *Urusei Yatsura*, the "Japanese" aspects of otaku culture are not connected to premodern Japan in any simple sense. Rather, those aspects should be perceived as emanating from a postwar Americanism (the logic of consumer society), which severed such historical continuities connecting the present with an ancient past. The insatiable appetite for parody manga at the Comiket or Comic Market[24] in the 1970s is closer to the urge that fueled pop art in the United States ten years earlier than to the Edo-period style. It is also no doubt more appropriate to see the artis-tic world of *Urusei Yatsura* as the infusion of Japanese motifs into a distorted science fiction and fantasy imaginary rather than as a direct offshoot of traditional Japanese folklore. Lurking at the foundations of otaku culture is the complex yearning to produce a *pseudo-Japan* once again from American-made material, after the destruction of the "good old Japan" through the defeat in World War II.

The form of otaku culture thus invites contradictory responses in the minds of many Japanese. Take, for example, the image of a young *miko* (a Shinto shrine maiden often depicted as a spiritual medium),

Figure 1a. Sailor Mars from *Sailor Moon*. Produced by Toei Animation.

which is consistent and highly popular in otaku novels and anime. There are an infinite number of works in which young women dressed in *miko* attire use special powers, turn into cyborgs, or fly on spaceships. The characters of Sakura from *Urusei Yatsura* and Sailor Mars from *Sailor Moon* are two such examples.[25]

Otaku older than a certain generation for some reason tend to divide into two clear groups when confronted with these sorts of images of female characters: one is excessively attracted to them and the other is excessively repulsed by them. And this division renders difficult any debate about otaku culture. The opposing reactions most likely originate from the difference in the way these two types of people encounter the combination of Japanese *miko* and Western fantasy motifs— those who feel an affinity for the existence of the *miko* even under the strong influence of Western fantasy, and those who harbor physiological disgust at the corruption of the pure Japanese existence of things such as *miko* by the imaginary of Western fantasy. In other words, the issue is whether or not one accepts the strangely warped image of Japan produced by otaku—in a sense a grotesque and disturbed imaginary that can create a *miko* holding a witch's broom, telling astrology, and wearing the uniform of a Japanese junior high school student.

Figure 1b. Sakura from *Urusei Yatsura*. Produced by Studio Pierrot.

Those who can embrace this hybrid imaginary as "Japanese" are able
to accept otaku works, and those who cannot find them unbearable.

The Scars of Defeat Underlying Japanese Culture

The obsession with Japan in otaku culture did not develop from Japanese tradition but rather emerged after this tradition had disappeared.
To put it another way, the trauma of defeat—that is, the harsh reality
that we had decisively lost any traditional identity—lies beneath the
existence of otaku culture. Those who reject the imaginary of otaku as
"horrifying" have in fact subconsciously reached this realization.

This is largely how I see the situation. Perhaps some readers may
be puzzled that I am dragging events that occurred more than fifty
years ago into a discussion on contemporary subculture. Yet the legacy
of World War II has determined the entire culture of Japan to a greater
extent than we imagine. Art critic Sawaraki Noi, for example, asserts
that contemporary art operated for a prolonged period within a "negative place" dictated by the war defeat and that artists themselves did not
face up to this situation until after the 1990s.[26] As most now realize,
until the 1980s Japanese society failed to face many of the contradictions

that emerged from the defeat and subsequent high economic growth, which meant that the resolution of these contradictions extended into the 1990s. And this phenomenon was reiterated even in various modes for expression.

The Postmodernism Fad and the Expansion of Otaku Culture

Once we have drawn our attention to these conditions, the cause of otaku's obsession with Japan can also be viewed from a different angle. While the term "otaku" was not broadly recognized until 1989, otaku became conscious of themselves as a group, and the previously mentioned pseudo-Japanese imaginary came to draw wide-ranging support, from the 1970s to the 1980s. This period, moreover, coincided almost directly with the coming into vogue of the intellectual trend known as "postmodernism." In 1983, the editor Nakamori Akio first used the term "otaku" in a commercial magazine. And in the same year, the economist Asada Akira published his bible on postmodernism, *Structure and Power (Kōzō to chikara).*[27]

Here I would like to make it clear that postmodern*ism* is a *different* concept from the previously discussed concept of postmodernity. The terms "postmodernity" or the "postmodern" here refer broadly to cultural conditions since the 1970s. Postmodernism, on the other hand, is a much narrower phrase pointing to a particular theoretical position (hence the suffix -*ism*). Suffice it to note that during the postmodern era a number of individual theories appeared, one of which is that body of thought that has been dubbed "postmodernism."

Theories of postmodernism emerged in France in the 1960s, spread to the United States in the 1970s, and were imported into Japan in the 1980s. Postmodernism is a complex and difficult discourse that grew out of an amalgamation of structuralism, Marxism, theories on consumer society, and critical theory. Its circulation was thus largely confined to universities. In Japan, however, it was acclaimed outside universities in the mid 1980s as a fashionable mode of thought for the younger generation, but then subsequently forgotten together with the era. As a fad in theory, Japanese postmodernism was often referred to as "New Academism."[28] Even after postmodernism (i.e., "New

Academism") disappeared from Japan, theories on postmodernism remained a subject of study in English language universities throughout
the world and affected subsequent academic trends. As I have written
on these differing circumstances in an earlier essay, I ask those who
are interested to consult that text.[29] In any case, what is important here
is not really the content of theories of postmodernism but the fact
that in Japan this highly complex body of thought turned into a kind
of faddish media frenzy.

As a few critics at the time have already pointed out,[30] this postmodernism fad was connected to the narcissism that permeated
Japanese society in the 1980s. The discourse on postmodernism popular in Japan at the time was unique in the way it deliberately confused
and intermingled questions over what encompassed "postmodernism"
and what encompassed "Japaneseness."

The claim endorsed by postmodernists at the time went something like this: Postmodernization refers to a process that occurs after
modernity. However, Japan was never completely modernized in the
first place. Until now this has been considered a defect; but as we
progress to a new stage of world history from modernity to postmodernity, it rather promises to become a benefit, because this nation, never
fully modernized, is easily able to embrace the process of postmodernization. For instance, as modern perceptions of humanity never
fully penetrated Japan, it can adapt to the collapse of the concept of
subjectivity with little resistance. In this way, Japan will emerge in the
twentieth century as a leading nation boasting a fully matured consumer society and technological prowess . . .

Whereas modernity equals the West, postmodernity equals Japan.
To be Japanese is thus to be standing at the forefront of history. Histor-
ically, this simplistic formula could be conceived as a repetition of the
claims of the prewar Kyoto School that Japan was able to "overcome
modernity."[31] Concurrently, it was also a direct reflection of the economic climate of the times. In the mid-1980s, in direct contrast to
the United States, which had been suffering a protracted period of
economic tumult since the Vietnam War, Japan suddenly stood at the
zenith of the world economy, having entered a period of short-lived
prosperity that would end in the bubble economy.

Postmodernists in Japan during this time elected to draw on the work of the French philosopher Alexandre Kojève.[32] Nothing better expresses the reality of Japanese postmodernists' desires than this choice. As I explain further in the following chapter, Kojève is known for ascertaining two different types of possible social formation in the postmodern era: the animalization of society as seen in the U.S. model and the spread of snobbery as illustrated in the Japanese model. In this regard, Kojève is oddly sympathetic toward Japan, and he predicts that the Japanization (or snobbery) of Westerners will prevail over Americanization (or animalization). In the eyes of Japanese in the 1980s, the prosperity of the times no doubt signified that we were heading toward the realization of this prospect.

Phrased another way, the prosperity of the 1980s enabled Japanese society to forget superficially the existence of its complex toward the United States, which we have examined. "Now the United States has been defeated! We no longer have to speak about the penetration of Americanism in Japan but rather must consider the advancement of Japanism in America!" The rise of postmodernism as an intellectual fad was supported by a climate that produced such claims. This same set of factors in turn aided the spread of otaku culture. The image of Japan that obsesses otaku is in fact no more than a U.S.-produced imitation, yet the atmosphere described above was the very thing that conveniently allowed people to forget about these origins.

The Illusion That Japan Is on the Cutting Edge

The anime *Megazone 23*, directed and written by Ishiguro Noboru and produced in 1985, can be cited as an example of an otaku work that reacted sensitively to the self-congratulatory atmosphere of those times. In the setting of the anime, contemporary Tokyo is in reality just a fiction created on a futuristic spaceship, a virtual reality constructed by a computer. As the narrative unfolds, the hero comes to realize the fictitiousness of this world and struggles to escape its confines. This setting alone is of profound interest, but more notable is a scene in the second half of the story, in which the protagonist asks the computer its reason for choosing the 1980s Tokyo as the stage for its fiction.

In answer to this somewhat metafictional question, the computer replies, "because for the people, it was the most peaceful era."[33] These lines no doubt struck a common chord not only with otaku but also with many of the younger generation living in Tokyo at the time. Japan in the 1980s was entirely a fiction. Yet this fiction, *while it lasted*, was comfortable to dwell in. This lightheartedness, as I understand it, was realized at the level of discourse in the fad of postmodernism and at the level of subculture in the expansion of otaku culture. This lightheartedness virtually disappeared in the 1990s, which began with the collapse of the bubble economy and was followed by the Kobe earthquake, the Aum sarin gas incident, and the emergence of issues like "compensated dating" and the breakdown of classroom order.[34] Yet it appears that the world of otaku culture is an exception; there the 1980s illusion has remained alive and well. For it was precisely from the 1990s onward that Japanese anime and video and computer games obtained international acclaim and the strength of these fields was widely recognized.

In fact, in readers familiar with the previous discourse of postmodernism, the claims of otaku commentators in the mid-1990s were so totally outmoded as to invoke a sense of nostalgia. For example, Okada suggests that "otaku culture may emerge as a major international trend" and Murakami that "perhaps Japan is the future of the world." These claims are very similar to Sakamoto Ryūichi's 1985 assertion that "for three to five hundred years there has never been a period where Japanism was as trendy as it is now. Even more so than the popularity of woodblock prints."[35] It may be said that discourse on otaku culture in this respect preserved the lighthearted playful atmosphere of the 1980s and donned a self-gratifying narcissism.

The Pseudo-Japan Manufactured from U.S.-made Material

So the relationship between "Japan" and otaku culture was torn more or less into two separate paths in the collective psyche. On the one hand, as connected to the experience of defeat, the presence of otaku culture is a grotesque reflection of the fragility of a Japanese identity.

This is because the "Japanese" themes and modes of expression created by otaku are in fact all imitations and distortions of U.S.-made material. On the other hand, the presence of this culture is connected to the narcissism of the 1980s and is also a fetish that can feed the illusion of Japan being at the cutting edge of the world. This is because, although the peculiar pseudo-Japan imaginary was created by otaku with the U.S.-made material, it has developed into an independent culture that is able to discount that influence.

This is the source of both extreme antagonism toward and over-glorification of otaku culture. Ultimately, at the root of both of these opposing positions lies extreme anxiety about the complete transformation of Japanese culture after the war by the wave of Americanization and consumer society. "A pseudo-Japan manufactured from U.S.-produced material" is now the only thing left in our grasp. We can only construct an image of the Japanese cityscape by picturing family restaurants, convenience stores, and "love hotels." And it is, moreover, within this impoverished premise that we have long exercised our distorted imaginary. For those who regard these conditions as unacceptable, otaku are detestable; conversely, those who overly identify with them end up becoming otaku. This is the mechanism that operates within Japanese subcultures. Precisely for this reason, those below a certain age group generally are sharply split into either otaku-philes or otaku-phobes.

I would like to cite one final example that illustrates clearly the condition of the pseudo-Japan favored by otaku. *Saber Marionette J* (*Seibā Marionetto Jei*, Shimoda Masami, 1996), originally written by Akahori Satoru, was a television anime series that first aired in 1996–97. At first glance, the series appears to be a cheap slapstick science fiction comedy, but for that very reason it in fact brilliantly depicts the structure of the otaku fantasy.

The work is set on an imaginary planet inhabited only by men. The only females present on the planet are androids called Marionettes. Yet all the men on the planet, too, are in fact mere clones made from several different original humans. Each separate clone group made from the same original has its own city-state governed by a clone heir. The city of "Japoness," a replica of Edo, forms the backdrop for the anime, which centers on the main character (a male hero) and three particular Marionettes who possess, because of a particular set of circumstances, "hearts."

Initially, the role of these three Marionette androids is concealed from the hero and the audience. However, halfway through the story, setting gradually becomes apparent. The planet on which the anime is set is a satellite colony of Earth and was originally supposed to include female clones as well. There are no females on the planet due to a computer mishap on the colony's ship. The only female originally on the ship is still preserved there in a frozen state, orbiting the sky around the planet. In order to salvage the girl from this state and bring her down to the planet's surface, the ship's computer, which has gone haywire and is keeping her in its custody, must be fooled into releasing her. Thus, a scheme has been put into place to create a virtual program that almost perfectly duplicates a human "heart" and input it as a replacement to the girl held captive. As the programmed "heart" is ultimately a fake, three other simulated programs are necessary in order to exchange them with the real thing. The Marionette androids that appear in the story have been made for this purpose. In other words, these female androids were in fact not merely substitutes for real women but were imitations made to exchange for the original—to be sacrificed in order to ensure the second coming of the female race. The hero's struggle begins upon learning this truth. He is faced with the key dilemma of having to choose between, on the one hand, the Marionettes who in fact only contain artificial personalities but who have been longtime companions and, on the other hand, someone said to possess the personality of a real human but who is a total stranger—between the imitation, which looks real, or the real thing, which has never been seen.

This story line is a brilliant allegory not only of the general issue of communication but also of the otaku worldview. Close at hand are characters who are merely imaginary creations but who are sufficiently sexual and to whom one can relate adequately. On the other hand, the real-life female is a distant presence, as far removed as an orbiting satellite. Even if this real female could be reached, at that point feelings for the imaginary characters that have been built up over a long period would have to be sacrificed in exchange for her. To otaku in the 1990s obsessed with "*chara-moe*," the various traits related to manga and anime characters and defined as desirable by otaku,[36] a phenomenon that will be analyzed at length in the following chapter, and particularly for male otaku who experienced the massive boom in girl games[37] and anime figurines, this dilemma no doubt seemed markedly true to life.

The Illusion of "Edo Merchant Culture"

Moreover, in the context of this chapter it is important to note that the place where otaku fantasies are played out is portrayed as a kind of theme park replica of Edo merchant culture. Japan's Edo period is frequently depicted, including in the work of Kojève, as an era when historical progress ceased and an introverted snobbery flourished. As revealed in the expression "Shōwa Genroku," people sought to favorably compare society at the end of Shōwa (i.e., in the 1980s) with the Edo period.[38] In the 1980s, the media frequently fed on postmodernists' theory on the significance of Edo.

The mechanism fueling this desire is easily understood. Japan's cultural traditions have been severed twice: during the Meiji Restoration and following defeat in World War II. In addition, memories of the period from Meiji to the 1945 defeat have been subject to political repression in the postwar period. If the narcissistic Japan of the 1980s was to forget defeat and remain oblivious to the impact of Americanization, it was easiest to return to the image of the Edo period. This kind of collective psychology lies behind frequent arguments that the Edo period was in fact already postmodern, including those otaku theories put forth by Ōtsuka and Okada.

Therefore, the "Edo" envisaged within such claims is, again, often not based on reality but rather comprises a form of fiction constructed in an effort to escape the impact of Americanization. The city of Japoness depicted in *Saber Marionette J* personifies the dubiousness of the kind of Edo-like imaginary recreated by otaku/postmodernists (see Figure 2). The spectacle of ultramodern technology mingled with

Figure 2. Otaku-like pseudo-Edo from *Saber Marionette J*. Produced by Sōtsū.

premodern everyday customs that form the backdrop to this anime is
totally lacking in any sense of reality. Due to the nature of TV anime,
the characters are designed with highly accentuated features and use
overly artificial emotional expressions. The castle of Japoness trans-
forms into a robot, and the costumes of the Marionettes, while mod-
eled on kimonos, have been altered in various ways to accentuate the
sex appeal of the female androids, resulting in attire resembling that
found in the *imekura* sex parlors.[39] Perhaps due to its low budget, the
anime also frequently recycles cells, and most of the male characters,
apart from the hero and a few others, can hardly be told apart. The
story line moreover is largely based on slapstick comedy, notably out of
place in the seriousness of the anime's setting. Both in terms of cine-
matography and narrative, this anime is without depth or consistency.
However, in a sense this is both a caricature of the otaku pseudo-Japan
and a caricature of the conditions of contemporary Japanese culture. I
do not think the producers consciously incorporated this subtext into
Saber Marionette J, but in this regard the work boasts a hidden inge-
nuity in clearly depicting the unique features of otaku culture.

The Significance of Otaku Culture

As is evident from the above discussion, the investigation of otaku culture in Japan amounts to more than a mere account of a subculture. In fact, it involves reflection on the issues of Japan's inability to come to terms with war defeat, of the American cultural invasion of Japan, and of the distorted conditions brought about through modernization and postmodernization. The study of otaku culture is, thus, also deeply tied to political and ideological issues. For instance, since the end of the Cold War, it could be said that right-wing Japanese discourse has generally survived by allowing itself to become subculturized, falsified, and otaku-ized. This process can be seen through the work of Kobayashi Yoshinori, Fukuda Kazuya, and Torihada Minoru.[40] The popularity of such figures, then, cannot be explained by merely tracing their assertions without considering the history of subculture in Japan. I am also deeply interested in this issue, which I hope to consider some time in the future.

Here my interest lies in another unique aspect of otaku culture, which in turn reaches beyond the framework of Japan and coincides with broader postmodern trends. Now that the importance of otaku culture has been explained, let us finally move on to the key issues at hand.

2. Database Animals

Otaku and Postmodernity

The Propagation of Simulacra

My claim that there is a deep relationship between the essence of otaku culture and postmodern social structure is not particularly new. The following two points have already been identified as postmodern characteristics of otaku culture.

One is the existence of *derivative works*. Here I use the phrase "derivative works" as a general term for the largely eroticized rereading and reproduction of original manga, anime, and games sold in the form of fanzines, fan games, fan figures, and the like. They are vigorously bought and sold mainly in the Comic Market (which meets twice a year in Tokyo), but also through countless small-scale exhibits held on the national level, and over the Internet. Founded by a base of amateurs, the market, where numerous copies circulate and a great number of professional authors get their start, formed the nucleus of otaku culture both quantitatively and qualitatively over the past twenty years. If we fail to consider the derivative works of amateurs in favor of only the commercially manufactured projects and products, we will be unable to grasp the trends of otaku culture.

This prominence of derivative works is considered a postmodern characteristic because the high value otaku place on such products is extremely close to the future of the culture industry as envisioned by French sociologist Jean Baudrillard. Baudrillard predicts that in postmodern society the distinction between original products and commodities and their copies weakens, while an interim form called the *simulacrum*, which is neither original nor copy, becomes dominant.[1] The discernment of value by otaku, who consume the original and the parody with equal vigor, certainly seems to move at the level of simulacra where there are no originals and no copies.

Furthermore, that transformation does not end with consumers. There have been many cases recently of best-selling authors who themselves produce and sell fanzines derivative of their own commercial products. For instance, it is well known that the original creator of *Sailor Moon* released products in the Comic Market. And, though they are not strictly derivative works, the company that produces *Evangelion* itself sells much software[2] that parodies the source. Here the distinctions between original and copy have already vanished even for the producer. Moreover, from the beginning the sense of realism in otaku genres has been weak; in many cases, even original works create worlds through citation and imitation of previous works. Without reference to the real world, the original is produced as a simulacrum of preceding works from the start, and in turn the simulacrum of that simulacrum is propagated by fan activities and consumed voraciously. In other words, irrespective of their having been created by an author (in the modern sense), the products of otaku culture are born into a chain of infinite imitations and piracy.

The Decline of the Grand Narrative

The second postmodern characteristic of otaku culture is the *importance placed on fiction* as a mode of action for the otaku. This attitude determines not only their hobby but also how they relate to people. In many cases, the human relations of the otaku, detached from the relations of workplace and family in the so-called social reality, are determined by an alternate principle for which fictional anime and games form the seed. The generation older than the otaku see this behavior only as retrograde, immature acts of the *moratoriamu*[3] period; this is the source of much friction.

The term "otaku" was born in the period from the 1970s to the 1980s when the otaku would refer to each other as "*otaku*."[4] Critic

Nakajima Azusa in his *Communication Deficiency Syndrome* argues that the essence of otaku is expressed in this alias. She notes: "What the word 'otaku' (meaning 'your home' or 'your family') points to is the assertion that one is identified, not by personal relations but by a relationship to the home unit and one's own territory." This kind of territory is necessary, according to Nakajima, because even after the paternal or national authority has been toppled, otaku must search for a group to which they should belong. The reason the otaku, "no matter where they go, cart around tons of books, magazines, fanzines, and scraps stuffed into huge paper bags like hermit crabs" is that, if they do not ferry around "the shell of their selves"—namely their fantasies of group affiliation—they cannot be mentally stable.[5] The personal pronoun *otaku* fulfills the function of mutually endorsing the fantasy of group affiliation. Nakajima's point is highly significant. For the otaku, certainly the fictional is taken far more seriously than social reality. And the media often conclude from this kind of observation that the otaku cannot distinguish between reality and games.

However, such a conclusion is imprudent. Since not all otaku are mental patients, it follows that they generally possess the ability to distinguish between fiction and reality. Their preference for fiction, as Nakajima explains, is related to their identity. The otaku choose fiction over social reality not because they cannot distinguish between them but rather as a result of having considered which is the more effective for their human relations, the value standards of social reality or those of fiction. For example, they choose fiction because it is more effective for smoothing out the process of communication between friends, reading the *Asahi Newspaper* and then going to vote, or lining up with anime magazines in hand for an exhibition. And, to that extent, it is they who may be said to be socially engaged and realistic in Japan today, by virtue of not choosing the "social reality." Otaku shut themselves into the hobby community not because they deny sociality but rather because, as social values and standards are already dysfunctional, they feel a pressing need to construct alternative values and standards.

This is a postmodern characteristic because the process by which the coexistence of countless smaller standards replace the loss of the singular and vast social standard corresponds precisely to the "decline

of the grand narrative"[6] first identified by the French philosopher Jean-
François Lyotard. From the end of eighteenth century to the mid-
twentieth century in modern countries, various systems were consoli-
dated for the purpose of organizing members of society into a unified
whole; this movement was a precondition for the management of society. These systems became expressed, for instance, intellectually as
the ideas of humanity and reason, politically as the nation-state and
revolutionary ideologies, and economically as the primacy of production. *Grand narrative* is a general term for these systems.

Modernity was ruled by the grand narrative. In contrast, in postmodernity the grand narratives break down and the cohesion of the
social entirety rapidly weakens. In Japan that weakening was acceler-
ated in the 1970s, when both high-speed economic growth and "the
season of politics" ended and when Japan experienced the Oil Shocks
and the United Red Army Incident.[7] From this vantage point, we can
view the otaku's neurotic construction of "shells of themselves" out of
materials from junk subcultures as a behavior pattern that arose to fill
the void from the loss of grand narrative.

On this point, sociologist Ōsawa Masachi's theory of otaku might
be useful. In his 1995 article "On Otaku" ("Otaku ron"), he claims
that, for the otaku, there is a "discord" in distinguishing between the
intrinsic other and the transcendental other; and for this reason otaku
are strongly attracted to the occult and mysticism.[8] This "distinction
between the intrinsic other and the transcendental other," put plainly,
means the distinction between the world of the other that surrounds
one's own self (the experiential world) and the godly world that transcends it (the transcendental world). The otaku cannot distinguish
between these two, with the result that they are easily hooked on
pseudoreligions that draw on themes popular in various subcultures.[9]
In a modern society, such disorder would have been dismissed as personal immaturity, but in postmodern society it is not so simple, because
the very society in which we live is something now characterized by
the "disorder" of the grand narrative. The behavioral pattern of the
otaku precisely reflects this characteristic of postmodernity. After having failed to grasp the significance of a "god" or "society" supported by
tradition, otaku try to fill the void with the subculture at their disposal.

In this way, otaku culture beautifully reflects the social structure of postmodernity on two points—the omnipresence of simulacra and the dysfunctionality of grand narrative. Studies on these two points are accumulating everywhere, so there is no need for me to add to them here. Consequently, here in chapter 2, I will pose two questions based on these two premises, which act as threads guiding otaku culture. In turn, these questions will help us to develop our consideration of the characteristics of postmodern society wherein they are intensified.

The two questions are:

1. In postmodernity, as the distinction between an original and a copy are extinguished, simulacra increase. If this is valid, then how do they increase? In modernity, the cause for the birth of an original was the concept of "the author." In postmodernity, what is the reason for the birth of the simulacra?

2. In postmodernity grand narratives are dysfunctional; "god" and "society," too, must be fabricated from junk subculture. If this is correct, how will human beings live in the world? In modernity, god and society secured humanity; the realization of this was borne by religious and educational institutions, but after the loss of the dominance of these institutions, what becomes of the humanity of human beings?

Narrative Consumption

Theory of Narrative Consumption

Let's begin with the first question. I would like first to draw attention to the previously mentioned *Theory of Narrative Consumption* by Ōtsuka Eiji. More than presuming the omnipresence of simulacra, Ōtsuka goes further in his analysis to consider the kind of logic under which simulacra are produced and consumed. Since I will draw heavily on Ōtsuka, I will cite him at length:

> Comics or toys are not consumed in and of themselves; rather, by virtue of the existence of an order behind these products or of a "grand narrative" of which they comprise a portion, each begins to take on value and to be consumed. So it becomes possible to sell countless

similar products (like the 772 different Bikkuriman stickers[10]), because consumers are led to believe that they themselves approach the overall picture of the "grand narrative." For example, the creators of lines of character "products" such as "Mobile Suit Gundam," "Saint Seiya," "Sylvanian Family," and "Onyanko Club" had prepared a "grand narrative" or an underlying order ahead of time, and this selling of concrete "goods" was directly tied to the consumers' knowledge of it.[11] ...

Interest in the program itself had been limited to a small group of enthusiasts, but in reality this has clearly become a shared feeling among consumers in certain areas, such as anime, comic, and toys. At this point we can see a new situation confronting today's consumer society. What is being consumed is not the individual "drama" or "goods" but rather the system hidden behind them. However, the system (or the grand narrative) itself cannot be sold, so, in appearance, installments of serialized dramas and "goods" get consumed as single fragments that are cross sections of the system. I want to label this kind of situation "narrative consumption" *(monogatari shōhi)*. . . .

However, products that presuppose this kind of "narrative consumption" have an extremely dangerous side. That is to say, if consumers through their cumulative consumption of "small narratives" get their hands on the entirety of the program that is a "grand narrative," they will freely manufacture "small narratives" with their own hands. For instance, let's consider the following case. Without the permission of the makers who hold the copyright, if someone exactly duplicates one of the Bikkuriman stickers of the 772 beginning with "Super Zeus," it is a crime. A sticker made in this way is a "knockoff." And to date there have been numerous incidents of this sort. On the other hand, what happens when the same person manufactures a 773rd character that is not drawn in the set of 772 stickers and, yet, is consistent with them and in accordance with the "worldview" of Bikkuriman? This is not a copy of any of the 772 originals. And therefore it is not a "knockoff" in that sense. Moreover, because it is consistent with the 772, the 773rd sticker has equal value to the original 772. At this phase of "narrative consumption" cases arise in which there is no distinction between the "real" (genuine, *honmono*) and the "fake" (knockoffs, *nisemono*) in these kinds of individual goods.[12]

From the Tree-model World to the Database-model World

Here Ōtsuka uses the phrase "small narrative" to mean a particular narrative within a particular work. By contrast, the "grand narrative"

supports that kind of small narrative, but the phrase also refers to the
"worldview" or "settings," which cannot be expressed by the surface of
a narrative.[13]

So according to Ōtsuka, each work in otaku culture merely functions as an entrance to this grand narrative. What consumers truly
value and buy are the settings and the worldview. Yet in reality, it is
difficult to sell settings and worldviews themselves as works. Therefore, a dual strategy is effected: although the actual commodities are
grand narratives, it happens to be small narratives, which are fragments
of grand narratives, that are sold as surrogate products. Ōtsuka labels
this situation *narrative consumption*. This is the natural consequence
of the inundation of simulacra known as derivative works.

More than an analysis of a subculture, this point is also suggestive of
a fundamental theory of postmodernity. To put it simply here, before
the arrival of the postmodern, in the era of modernity—when the grand
narrative was still functioning—the world could be grasped, roughly,
through a kind of *tree model* (or projection model) like the one given in
Figure 3a. On the one hand, there is the surface outer layer of the world
that is reflected in our consciousness. On the other hand, there is the
deep inner layer, which is equal to the grand narrative that regulates
the surface outer layer. In modernity it came to be thought that the
purpose of scholarship was to clarify the structure of the hidden layer.

However, with the arrival of postmodernity, that tree-model world
image collapsed completely. So what kind of structure accrues to the
postmodern world? One candidate for explaining the Japan of the
1980s that often seemed borne out in reality was the "rhizome" model,
in which signs are linked in diverse patterns over the outer layer alone
(the deep inner layer having been extinguished).[14] However, in my
mind, it is easier to comprehend the postmodern world through a
database model (or a reading-up[15] model) such as the one in Figure 3b.

An easily understandable example of this is the Internet. The Net
has no center. That is to say, no hidden grand narrative regulates all
Web pages. However, it is not a world established through the combination of outer signs alone, as in the case of the rhizome model. On
the Internet, rather, there is distinct *double-layer structure*, wherein, on
the one hand, there is an accumulation of encoded information, and,

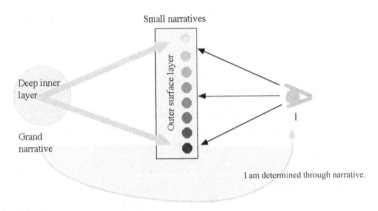

Figure 3a. The modern world image (the "tree" model).

on the other hand, there are individual Web pages made in accordance with the users "reading them up." The major difference between this double-layer structure and the modern tree model is that, with the double-layer structure, the agency that determines the appearance that emerges on the surface outer layer resides on the surface itself rather than in the deep inner layer; i.e., it belongs on the side of the user who is doing the "reading up," rather than with the hidden information itself. In the world of the modern tree model, the surface outer layer is determined by the deep inner layer, but in the world of the postmodern database model, the surface outer layer is not determined by the deep inner layer; the surface reveals different expressions at those numerous moments of "reading up."

For me, the shift in models is not simply a social shift, such as with the emergence of the Internet, but also was clearly demonstrated in the scholarly world by the ideas of complex systems theory, such as the self-organization of molecules, artificial life, or neural nets, that became widely known in the 1990s. However, I need not go into the details of postmodern theory here. For the purpose of following the argument, it is enough to say that the tree-model world image that is characteristic of modernity stands in opposition to the database model of the postmodern world image; in the deep inner layer of the former there is a grand narrative, but in the deep inner layer of the latter there is not.

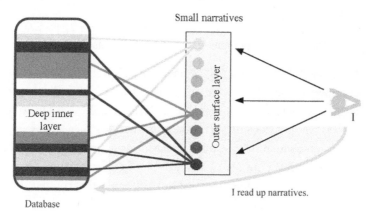

Figure 3b. The postmodern world image (the "database" model).

Rereading the aforementioned Ōtsuka chapter with the above premise in mind, we can see that the structure of the database model clearly reflects Ōtsuka's structure of narrative consumption. The dual structure of settings and small narratives represents the double-layer structure of information and appearance. In otaku culture ruled by narrative consumption, products have no independent value; they are judged by the quality of the database in the background. So, as these databases display various expressions depending on the differing modes of "reading up" by users, consumers, once they are able to possess the settings, can produce any number of derivative works that differ from the originals. If we think of this situation as occurring only in the surface outer layer, the original product or work can seem swallowed by the chaos of a sea of simulacra. However, in reality, it is better to assume the prior existence of a database (i.e., settings) that enables both an original and the works derived from it, depending on how one "reads up" the database.

That is to say, the otaku consumers, who are extremely sensitive to the double-layer structure of postmodernity, clearly distinguish between *the surface outer layer within which dwell simulacra,* i.e., the works, and *the deep inner layer within which dwells the database,* i.e., settings. Since this double-layer structure will appear many times in what follows, I want to emphasize the point here.

The Grand Nonnarrative

The Decline of the Grand Narrative and Fiction as Supplement

Even now, Ōtsuka's point has not fundamentally lost its validity. However, here I would like to add one amendment. Ōtsuka calls the settings or worldview a "grand narrative." The reason he uses this word, besides the influence of postmodernism that was then in vogue, is that it was common to discover a worldview or a historical view in the otaku products of the late 1980s. Take *Gundam,* for example: since its first television series was broadcast in 1979, works that continued the series, such as *Mobile Suit Z(eta) Gundam, Char's Counterattack,* and *Mobile Suit Double Z Gundam,* were conceived of as belonging to the same fictitious history. Accordingly, the desires of *Gundam* fans necessarily and faithfully embarked on a close examination of this fanciful history; in reality *Gundam*-related books were already shrouded in timelines and mechanical data. Certainly, as Nakajima Azusa has pointed out, at this point a narrative other than reality (i.e., fiction) is constructed.

And the fictional narrative occasionally fulfills the grand role of substituting for the real grand narrative (namely, political ideology). One of the most spectacular examples of this is Aum Shinrikyō, which equipped its doctrines with a subculture imagination and turned ultimately to terrorism.[16] As Ōsawa Masachi explicated in his *The End of the Fictional Age,*[17] the United Red Army of the 1970s and the Aum Shinrikyō of the 1990s differ only in that the former believed in communism, a widely recognized narrative, while the latter believed in a narrative that was still having difficulty winning broad recognition.

In the narrative consumption of the 1980s, too, social circumstances appeared in the background. As a reason for the rise of narrative consumption, Ōtsuka himself points to the extinguishing of "death" or the "mystical underworld" in modern society—that is to say, he points to the extinguishing of the transcendental.[18] Consequently, it is entirely appropriate for him to label the aggregate of worldview and settings supporting a subculture as a "grand narrative," because, in the situation of the 1980s, it must have seemed that the worldview and settings were constructed in order to compensate for the loss of grand narrative.

From Ideology to Fiction

The mechanism that compensates for the decline of grand narrative can be placed in a slightly broader framework. The latter half of the twentieth century (not just in Japan, but globally) was a time of grand change caught between two periods. The world until the 1950s was under the sway of the modern cultural logic, which could be grasped in the form of the tree model. Accordingly, grand narratives were constantly produced, indoctrinated, and desired. An example of this would be the students' immersion into leftist politics.

However, things began greatly to change in the 1960s; from the 1970s, the cultural logic of postmodernism strengthened rapidly. Consequently, grand narratives were already neither produced nor desired. Nevertheless, this kind of change placed a huge burden on the people who came to maturity at this moment. In spite of the global move toward a database model, they were planted with the old tree model (the desire for a grand narrative) in educational institutions and through written works. As a result of this paradox, this particular generation was driven to forge the grand narrative that had been lost. And though I will not elaborate further here, the interest in occult thought and New Age science that grew in America during the 1970s and the global radicalization of the student movements can be seen as results of this drive. The rise of otaku culture in Japan, too, of course shares the same social background. For the first-generation otaku who appeared at that time, knowledge of comics and anime or fan activities played a role extremely similar to the role played by the leftist thought and activism for the All-Campus Joint Struggle generation.[19]

The Appearance of a Generation Disinterested in Grand Narratives

Whether that kind of complex psychology regulates otaku culture even now is a different problem. I think, conversely, that with the evolution from the modern to the postmodern, the necessity for this kind of forgery had to fade. The younger generations that grew up within the postmodern world image imagine the world as a database from the beginning, since they do not need a perspective on the entire world that surveys all—that is to say, *they have no need for forgeries, even as a subculture.* And if this is the case, in the shift from the generation that needed fiction as a substitute for lost grand narratives to the generation that consumes fictions without such a need—even though they are two parts of the same otaku culture—then a grand transformation is realized in their forms of expression and consumption.

This new tendency became apparent in the 1990s, after the release of Ōtsuka's critique. Compared with the 1980s otaku, those of the 1990s generally adhered to the data and facts of the fictional worlds and were altogether unconcerned with a meaning and message that might have been communicated. Independently and without relation to an original narrative, consumers in the 1990s consumed only such fragmentary illustrations or settings; and this different type of consumption appeared when the individual consumer empathy toward these fragments strengthened. The otaku themselves called this new consumer behavior "*chara-moe*"—the feeling of *moe* toward characters and their alluring characteristics. As previously mentioned, here the otaku coolly consumed only the information that was behind the works without relation to the narrative or message of those works. Consequently, any scheme for analyzing this consumer behavior that proposes that these fragmentary works had already compensated for "the loss of grand narrative" is not really appropriate.

What the *Evangelion* Fans Wanted

Let's consider this through some concrete examples. I've already touched on *Mobile Suit Gundam.* In the 1990s, *Neon Genesis Evangelion* was frequently compared to *Gundam.* Both are science fiction anime with similar protagonists: young boys caught up in battles in the near future. These works were also widely supported by a generation close to that of the respective protagonist, even becoming a topic of conversation for the entire society. However, in reality, both *Neon Genesis Evange-*

lion and *Gundam* can be thought of as works that were consumed and supported by fans with entirely different attitudes about narratives.[20]

As described above, numerous fans of *Gundam* desired the completion and close examination of a singular *Gundam* world. That is to say, in their case they preserved the current passion for a fictitious grand narrative. However, even during the peak of the craze, the fans of *Evangelion* who appeared in the mid-1990s—especially those of the younger generation (the third generation of otaku)—did not really have a concern for the entire world of *Evangelion*. Instead they focused exclusively on the settings and character designs as objects for excessive interpretation or "reading up" (exemplified in derivative works), and for *chara-moe*.

For them, a grand narrative or fiction with a *Gundam*-style world was no longer desirable, even as a fantasy. *Gundam* fans' extraordinary adherence to the consistency of the timeline of the "space century" or to mechanical reality is well known. By contrast, many *Evangelion* fans required settings to empathize with the story's protagonist, to draw erotic illustrations of the heroine, and to build enormous robot figures, and showed obsessive interest in data to that extent, but beyond that they seldom immersed themselves into the world of the works.

This shift clearly appears again not only on the side of the consumers or the creators of derivative works but also from the point of view of the original creators. The first television broadcast of *Gundam* in 1979 was followed by several well-known sequels. Most of those were developed along the lines of a single fictitious history under the supervision of the general director, Tomino Yoshiyuki. In the case of *Evangelion*, however, there were no sequels and no plans to make sequels.[21] Instead, the original creator's production company, Gainax, developed the derivative works sold in the Comic Market and at the same time created plans for related concepts; for instance, there are mahjong games, erotic telephone card designs using the *Evangelion* characters, and even simulation games in which players nurture the heroine Ayanami Rei. These are all far removed from the originals.

The important point here is that this change exercised a strong influence on the structure of the original itself, as well as on the recycling of the originals and the related projects. In contrast to the *Gundam* director Tomino, Anno Hideaki (the director of *Evangelion*) antici- pated the appearance of derivative works in the Comic Market from the beginning, setting up various gimmicks within the originals to promote those products. For instance, a scene from a parallel *Evange- lion* world is inserted in the final episode of the television series. In that parallel world with a completely different history, an Ayanami Rei dwells with a completely different personality. But in fact the scene depicted there was already a parody of an image that had been widely circulated as a derivative work at the time of the original broadcast. That is to say, an extremely warped relationship is inter- woven into this work, where the original simulates in advance the simulacra.

Although two versions of this work were released for the cinema, both were framed as more than direct continuations of the television series, reworking the story with different versions of that fictional world. This characteristic is apparent in the 1997 *Evangelion Death*, which was made as an omnibus edition. This omnibus edition trans- forms video images from the TV series into the raw materials for remixing, presenting them as fragments without a unified narrative.

All of these characteristics indicate that, from the outset, the anime *Evangelion* was launched not as a privileged original but as a simulacrum at the same level as derivative works. In other words, this thing that Gainax was offering was certainly more than a single grand narrative, with the TV series as an entrance. Rather, it was an aggre- gate of information without a narrative, into which all viewers could empathize of their own accord and each could read up convenient narratives.

I call this realm that exists behind small narratives but lacks any form of narrativity *a grand nonnarrative*, in contrast to Ōtsuka's "grand narrative." Many consumers of *Evangelion* neither appreciate a com- plete anime as a work (in the traditional mode of consumption) nor consume a worldview in the background as in *Gundam* (in narrative consumption): from the beginning they need only nonnarratives or information.

Moe-elements

Narratives and Coffee Mugs as the Same Class of Merchandise

One might argue that the original TV series of *Evangelion* continued to function as *an entry into the database*, if not into a grand narrative. However, otaku culture of the few years since *Evangelion* is rapidly abandoning the need for even this kind of an entry point. The rise of multimedia plays an important role here. In today's market for otaku culture, the previously accepted order is no longer dominant; no more do original comics versions debut, followed by anime releases, and finally the related products and fanzines. For example, a proposal for an anime series may make its way into a PC game, and even before the anime production is complete it garners fan support through radio dramatizations and fan events, and even spawns related products that hit the market. Or, conversely, the commercial success of a PC game or trading cards could lead to the publication of fan anthologies (a collection of derivative works made with the permission of the original author) or novelizations, with the anime and comic versions only following later. There are multiple layers of these kinds of intricate circuits. In such a situation, it is quite ambiguous what the original is or who the original author is, and the consumers rarely become aware of the author or the original. For them, the distinction between the original and the spin-off products (as copies) does not exist; the only valid distinction for them is between the settings created anonymously (a database at a deep inner layer) and the individual works that each artist has concretized from the information (a simulacrum on the surface outer layer). Here, even the idea that the original functions as an entry point into the settings or the worldview is becoming inappropriate.

The most important example in understanding this trend is the character called Di Gi Charat or Digiko, created in 1998 (Figure 4). This character was originally created as a mascot for a dealer of anime- and gaming-related products. Therefore, no narratives existed behind it. However, the character gradually gained popularity in the latter half of 1998, broke out as a TV commercial in 1999, followed by anime and novels in 2000, and has established a solid world of its own.

Figure 4. *Di Gi Charat.*

What is noteworthy in this process is that the stories and settings that form its world were created collectively and anonymously as a response to the market, after the character design of Digiko alone gained support. For example, Usada Hikaru (or Rabi~en~Rose) and Petit Charat are characters associated with Digiko, but they were released only in 1999, and even the name of the former was decided by a fan poll (Figure 5). Furthermore, although Digiko is now known to be "cocky and carefree," these settings did not exist from the start but were added in the anime version as a sort of self-parody.

Moreover, unlike *Evangelion*, this development was not managed by a particular author or production company, because it was just part

Figure 5. Usada Hikaru (Rabi~en~Rose) and Petit Charat. *Di Gi Charat.* Produced by Broccoli.

of a corporate ad campaign. In such a situation, it does not make sense to ask what the original of Di Gi Charat is, who the author is, or what kind of message is implied. The entire project was driven by the power of fragments; projects such as the anime or the novel, formerly discussed independently as a "work," are merely related products, just like character mugs and loose-leaf binders. The narrative is only a surplus item, added to the settings and illustrations (the nonnarrative).

Combinations of *Moe*-elements

Another interesting point is that Di Gi Charat uses excessively advanced skill to trigger *chara-moe,* as if to compensate for the absence
of story and message. I wrote earlier that the design of Digiko alone
found support at first. However, one cannot quite say that the design
was particularly original or attractive. In fact, the design of Digiko is a
result of sampling and combining popular elements from recent otaku
culture, as if to downplay the authorship of the designer. I have identified some of the major elements in Figure 6.

I will not describe the characteristics of each element here, but
note that each element, with its own origins and background, constitutes a category that has been developed in order to stimulate the interest of the consumers. It is not a simple fetish object, but a sign that
emerged through market principles. For example, it is well known
that the "maid costume" originated in the X-rated anime series *Cream
Lemon: Black Cat Mansion* in the 1980s and gained popularity in the
"visual novels" of the 1990s.[22] Also, in my observation "hair springing
up like an antennae" was popularized in the visual novel *The Scar
(Kizuato)* (Figure 7), and it has become a standard element seen in
anime and games. From this point on, let us call these elements, developed to effectively stimulate the *moe* of the consumers, "*moe*-
elements" *(moe yōso).* Most of the *moe*-elements are visual, but there
are other kinds of *moe*-elements, such as a particular way of speaking,
settings, stereotypical narrative development, and the specific curves
of a figurine.

As one can immediately see in specialty stores in the Akihabara or
Shinjuku parts of Tokyo, the *moe*-elements are proliferating within
otaku culture. The "characters" circulating in these stores are not unique
designs created by the individual talent of the author but an output
generated from preregistered elements and combined according to
the marketing program of each work.

The otaku themselves are aware of this situation. The otaku search
engine "TINAMI" launched in 1996 signifies this awareness with an
actual device (Figure 8).[23] To enable the user to find illustrations from

hair sticking up like antennae

cat ears

bells

green hair

maid uniform

tail

big, loose socks

Figure 6. *Moe*-elements that constitute Di Gi Charat.

tens of thousands of registered sites, this searchable database classifies and quantifies various characteristics of otaku illustrations in detail. The site is equipped with selectable parameters so that the user can search for *moe*-elements. That is to say, the user can search for the desired characteristics of things like "cat ears" and "maid costumes," or can set "the percentage of characters appearing" at more than 75 percent, "the age of character" at between 10 and 15, and "the degree of déformé" at 5 in order to find desired characters categorized in the database. Figure 9 shows the actual search window of "TINAMI."

Figure 7. An "antenna hair" as a *moe*-element seen in *The Scar (Kizuato)*.
Produced by Leaf.

Some of the "categories" lined up at the bottom half of the figure are
moe-elements, such as "cat ears," "animal," "angels," "maid costumes,"
and "glasses."

As the Internet spread and the site of otaku activities moved to the
Web during the late 1990s, search engines such as "TINAMI" began
to play a prominent role. In such an environment, the producers, like
it or not, must have been conscious of their position relative to the

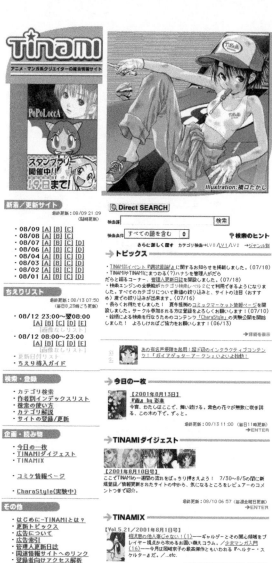

Figure 8. TINAMI homepage.

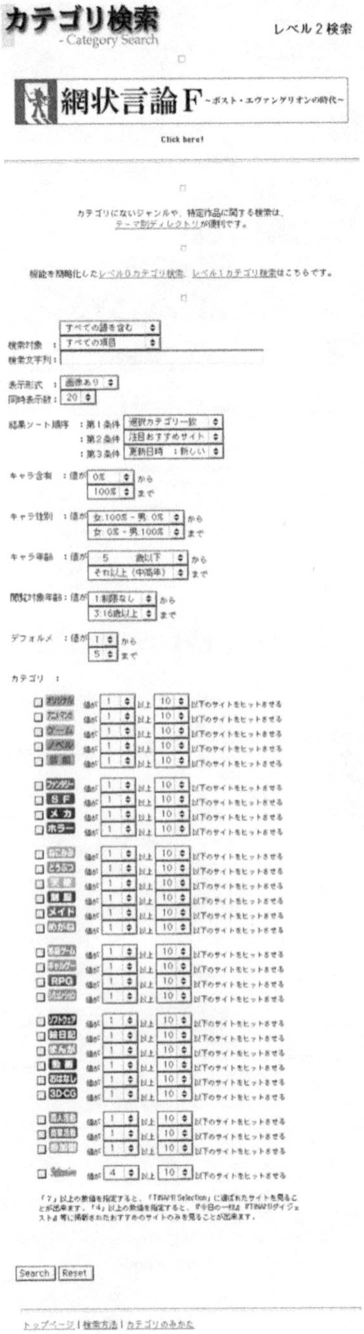

Figure 9. TINAMI search screen.

whole of otaku culture. As soon as the characters are created, they are broken up into elements, categorized, and registered to a database. If there is no appropriate classification, a new element or category simply will be added. In this sense, the originality of an "original" character can only exist as a simulacrum.

There used to be a narrative behind a work. But as the importance of narrative has declined, the characters have become more important in otaku culture. Subsequently, a database for *moe*-elements that generates the characters has been established. Otaku culture of the 1990s has followed this general trend, but *Di Gi Charat*, which emerged at the end of the 1990s, marks the terminal point of this trend.

In fact, the characters in this work were created with intentionally excessive *moe*-elements. The novelization describes Digiko as having "the maid costume with lots of frills, a cap with white cat ears, cat gloves, cat boots, and a cat tail. Perfect and fully equipped with double-*moe*-options," while Puchiko is described as wearing "a tiger-striped hat with cat ears, a girls' school uniform ('sailor suits') and bloomers, a tiger cat tail. A double-*moe* costume, quite evil and foul for fans."[24] These self-parodying descriptions clearly indicate the fragile position of this work. Digiko has cat ears and speaks with "-*nyo*" (the Japanese sound for "meow") at the end of her sentences.[25] This is not because cat ears or the "-*nyo*" endings are exactly attractive themselves, but because both cat ears and peculiar sentence endings are *moe*-elements and, to be exact, because the otaku of the 1990s accepted them as *moe*-elements as they became aware of the whole structure of this process. In this sense, *Di Gi Charat* is not so much a project that naively relies on the desire of *chara-moe* but a complex project that, by pushing that desire to the limit, has become a satire for the present market dominated by *moe*-related designs.

Database Consumption

Attractive Characters, Rather Than Quality of Individual Works

The organization of the *moe*-elements has rapidly advanced in the 1990s. The term *moe* is said to have emerged in the late 1980s, originally referring to the fictional desire for characters of comics, anime, and games or for pop idols. Since those who feel *moe* toward a particular character tend to buy its related goods excessively, the success of a project for the producers of such goods is directly determined not by the quality of the work itself but by its ability to evoke the *moe* desire through character design and illustrations. This tendency goes back to the 1970s, but its significance decisively increased in the context of the 1990s multimedia trend.

With the new multimedia, various kinds of projects can progress simultaneously while leaving the status of the original quite ambiguous. Therefore, the common ground for all of these projects is neither the authorship of the original creator nor a message but a common world of the work and characters, or, in extreme cases, characters alone. For example, the only reason (other than copyright) for categorizing the TV and film series *Evangelion,* directed by Anno Hideaki, with the "nurturing"[26] simulation game *Ayanami Nurturing Project* as "*Evangelion*-connected" works, or categorizing novel games such as *Droplet* ("*Shizuku*") and *The Scar* ("*Kizuato*") created by Leaf and its parodied trading card game *Leaf Fight* as "Leaf-connected" works is that they feature the same characters. Since the continuity in terms of content between these works is extremely weak, the fans of *Evangelion* and *Droplet* could very well have shown little interest in *Ayanami Nurturing Project* or *Leaf Fight.* Such consumer behavior could have been dominant; it even would have been easier to understand outside of the otaku market.

But the otaku market of the 1990s systematically raised consumers who accepted both versions within a single spectrum and, in fact, the market expanded its size on the basis of the inundation of such "related goods." As a result, instead of narratives creating characters, it has become a general strategy to create character settings first, followed by works and projects, *including the stories.* Given this situation, the attractiveness of characters is more important than the degree of perfection of individual works, and the know-how for enhancing the attractiveness (through the art of the *moe*-element) has rapidly accumulated. Under such circumstances, the development of *moe*-element databases has become a necessity.

Connections between Characters across Individual Works

As a result, many of the otaku characters created in recent years are connected to many characters across individual works, rather than emerging from a single author or a work. For example, Figure 10 lists four characters: Hoshino Ruri from *Martian Successor Nadesico,* Ayanami Rei from *Evangelion,* Tsukishima Ruriko from *Droplet,* and Ōtorii Tsubame from *Cyber Team in Akihabara (Akihabara Dennōgumi).* These characters have many things in common in terms of settings and designs.

Such connections, frequently seen in otaku works, have been called "quotations," "influences," and "parodies." However, notions such as "quotations" and "influences" unconsciously presuppose a unit such as an author or a work. For example, there is a notion that an author is influenced by another author's work, and he or she quotes it or sometimes parodies it. Even now we can say that the activities of otaku works lie within such a model. For example, it is not incorrect to trace the genealogy of our four characters as follows: Ruriko was created

Figure 10a. Hoshino Ruri. Designed by Gotō Keiji. *Martian Successor Nadesico.* Produced by XEBEC.

Figure 10b. Ayanami Rei. Designed by Sadamoto Yoshiyuki. *Neon Genesis Evangelion.* Produced by Gainax.

under the influence of Rei, and Ruri was created as quotations from both, and Tsubame is a parody of Ruri.

However, the validity of this model is limited. Let us say that Ruri is a quotation of Rei or Ruriko. But who did the quoting? In comparison with *Evangelion,* where the roles of Anno as a director and Sadamoto Yoshiyuki[27] as a character designer were relatively clear, it is difficult to determine the involvement of Sato Tatsuo and Mamiya Kia in the complex production process of *Nadesico.*[28] Moreover, the example in Figure 10 is just a tip of the iceberg.

Figure 10c. Tsukishima Ruriko. Designed by Minazuki Tōru. *Droplet*. Produced by Leaf.

In fact, in the late 1990s, characters bearing a close resemblance to Ayanami Rei have been produced and consumed on a massive scale— in comics, anime, and novelizations, both in the commercial market and the fanzine market. It does not seem wise to attribute this expanse to the "influence" of *Evangelion*.

I believe that it is more appropriate to use the image of the database to grasp this current situation. The emergence of Ayanami Rei did not influence many authors so much as change the rules of the *moe*-elements sustaining otaku culture. As a result, even those authors who were not deliberately thinking of *Evangelion* unconsciously began

Figure 10d. Ōtorii Tsubame. Designed by Kotobuki Tsukasa. *Cyber Team in Akihabara.* Produced by Ashi Production.

to produce characters closely resembling Rei, using newly registered *moe*-elements (quiet personality, blue hair, white skin, mysterious power). Such a model is close to the reality of the late 1990s. Beyond Rei, characters emerging in otaku works were not unique to individual works but were immediately broken into *moe*-elements and recorded by consumers, and then the elements reemerged later as material for creating new characters. Therefore, each time a popular character appeared, the *moe*-element database changed accordingly, and as a result, in the next season there were heated battles among the new generation of characters featuring new *moe*-elements.

The Double-layer Structure of Consumption as Seen in *Chara-moe*

As these observations make clear, the *chara-moe,* which represents otaku culture of the 1990s, is not the simple act of empathy (as the otaku themselves wish to believe). It is a quite postmodern consumer behavior, sustained by the movements back and forth between the characters (the simulacra) and the *moe*-elements (the database). Within the consumer behavior of feeling *moe* for a specific character, along with the blind obsession, there is hidden a peculiarly cool, detached dimension—one that takes apart the object into *moe*-elements and objectifies them within a database. I will discuss this double-layer structure in detail below, with visual novels as an example, but suffice it to say that *chara-moe* cannot be explained away merely as a fanatical consumer behavior.

The otaku's *moe* sensibility is doubled between the level of individual characters and the level of *moe*-elements, and that is exactly why the otaku are able to swap the objects of the *moe* so quickly. If the otaku were selecting the characters simply according to their own tastes without the level of *moe*-elements, then the fans of each character would be unrelated to those of another character. If this had been the case, then the "character business" that bloomed in the 1990s would not have been possible.

From "Narrative Consumption" to "Database Consumption"

To summarize the discussion up to this point, there is no longer a narrative in the deep inner layer, beneath the works and products such as comics, anime, games, novels, illustrations, trading cards, figurines, and so on. In the multimedia environment of the 1990s, it is only characters that unite various works and products. The consumer, knowing this, moves easily back and forth between projects with a narrative (comics, anime, novels) and projects without one (illustrations and figurines). Here, the individual projects are the simulacra and behind them is the database of characters and settings.

At yet another level, however, each character is merely a simulacrum, derived from the database of *moe*-elements. In other words, the double-layer structure of the simulacra and the database is again doubled, forming a complex system. The otaku first consume individual works, and sometimes are moved by them. But they are also aware that, in fact, the works are merely simulacra, consisting only of the characters. Then they consume characters, and sometimes feel *moe* in them. But they are also aware that, in fact, the characters are just simulacra, consisting only of combinations of *moe*-elements. In my observation, *Di Gi Charat* is a project created with a high degree of self-awareness of the doubled (and perhaps even tripled) consciousness of the otaku.

Therefore, to consume *Di Gi Charat* is not simply to consume a work (a small narrative) or a worldview behind it (a grand narrative), nor to consume characters and settings (a grand nonnarrative). Rather, it is linked to consuming the database of otaku culture as a whole. I call this consumer behavior *database consumption,* in contrast with Ōtsuka's "narrative consumption."

In the shift from modernity to postmodernity, our world image is experiencing a sea change, from one sustained by a narrative-like, cinematic perspective on the entire world to one read-up by search engines, characterized by databases and interfaces. Amid this change, the Japanese otaku lost the grand narrative in the 1970s, learned to fabricate the lost grand narrative in the 1980s (narrative consumption), and in the 1990s, abandoned the necessity for even such fabrication and learned simply to desire the database (database consumption). Roughly speaking, such a trend may be surmised from Ōtsuka's critical essay and my own observation. Figure 11 shows the difference between narrative consumption and database consumption. Figures 11a and 11b correspond to the aforementioned Figures 3a and 3b, respectively.

The Novels of "Anime/Manga-like Realism"

It is unavoidable that many examples of otaku culture are visually oriented, but let me cite a different example of how the rise of the *chara-moe* and database consumption is beginning to exert tremendous influence on print culture. In the mass media, the "novel" is still categorized as either "literature" or "entertainment." In reality, however, for ten years the otaku market has been producing and consuming numerous novels

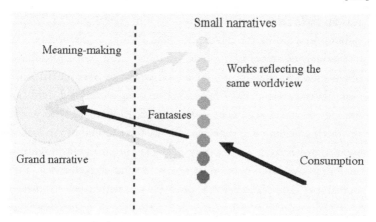

Figure 11a. The structure of narrative consumption.

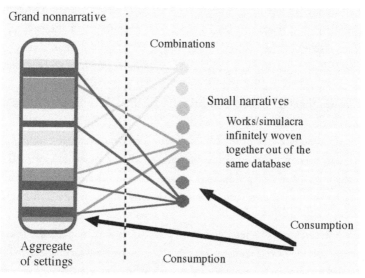

Figure 11b. The structure of database consumption.

that cannot be classified as either. Sometimes labeled with existing categories such as "mystery," "science fiction," and "fantasy" and sometimes labeled in with reference to their readership or producers such was "junior novels," "game novels," and "young adult (juvenile)," these works have a fictional world with a unique logic that differs from the traditional classification as either literary or entertaining. For this reason, their general reputation is poor. But their logic can be naturally understood in the context of otaku culture, as discussed above.

Perhaps the most appropriate example of this new and different breed of novels may be found in the works of Seiryōin Ryūsui.[29] Seiryōin was born in 1974, falling between the second and third generations of otaku. His debut novel, *Cosmic* (1996), is a mystery novel in which a dozen or so detectives try to solve several dozen locked-room murder cases. That setting is already original, but in addition each detective is given an impressive name and characteristics: Yaiba Somahito ("The Blade Wizard"), who reasons with a dialectic method called "Jin-suiri" ("Syn-llogism"); Tsukumo Jūku ("Ninety-nine Nineteen"), who uses intuition called "Jintsū Riki" ("Divine wisdom and cosmology"); and Amagiri Fuyuka ("Rain-mist Winter-aroma"), who speculates in her sleep, a talent referred to as "Gori Muchū" (Enlightenment and reason in the dream). The resolutions of the mysteries are also extremely absurd. In addition, these superhuman characters appear in a subsequent series of novels, including *Joker, Jukebox*, and *Carnival*.[30] Since his debut, Seiryōin has been declaring that these novels together form a "Great Story of the Water Stream" ("*Ryūsui Taisetsu*").[31] In short, his novels may not emphasize the quality of an individual work, but they contribute to the attractiveness of individual characters and consequently the quality of "the Seiryōin world" that they constitute as a series. This author consistently has garnered strong support among teenagers, but some veteran mystery writers have reacted negatively.

Referring to Ōtsuka again, he points out that, behind the rise of this sort of novel, realism itself has begun to transform itself.[32] The modern Japanese novel is said to reflect reality vividly *(shasei);* the otaku novel reflects fiction vividly.[33] The characters and stories that Seiryōin depict are never realistic, but they are possible in the world of comics and anime already published, and therefore the reader accepts them as real. Ōtsuka called such an attitude "anime/manga-like Realism" and identified its origin in the science fiction writer Arai Motoko's statement at the end of the 1970s that she "wanted to write the print version of the comics *Lupin the Third*." Ōtsuka argues that, although the naturalistic realism (of the modern Japanese novel) and the "anime/manga-like Realism" give very different impressions on surface, the progression from the former to the latter was a matter of necessity, because in Japan the former was fictional to begin with.

Elements of Mystery Fiction as *Moe*-elements

Once again, I agree with Ōtsuka's observation in general, but I must emphasize that the very fiction supposed to be "reflected vividly" has already been broken up into individual elements and collected in the database. It is well known that Seiryōin's novels are influenced by Kurumada Masami's popular manga *Saint Seiya*. At the same time, Seiryōin constructs his world by extracting and freely combining various elements from the all of the numerous neo-orthodox mystery novels of the mid-1980s to mid-1990s. Here, the reader shares the same database. That the author can quickly write dozens of discernibly different locked-room murder mysteries with a dozen or so different detectives—and that the readers accept it as a matter of course—is only possible because images of detectives, tricks, and ways of solving mysteries have already become *moe*-elements.

Such self-referential awareness of the conditions of the genre is probably inherited from the writers of a previous generation, such as Ayatsuji Yukito and Norizuki Rintarō.[34] But one great distinction is that, where the previous generation directed their consciousness to the rules (codes) of mystery,[35] Seiryōin's consciousness is directed toward the database of *moe*-elements. It is commonly accepted that the market for mystery greatly expanded in the 1990s, but as far as the young readership is concerned, such growth was sustained by readers differing from the "orthodox" fans who enjoyed clever tricks; the new readers felt *moe* toward characters created by Kyōgoku Natsuhiko and Mori Hiroshi,[36] drew illustrations of them, and embarked on derivative works from them.

This situation spreads beyond the mystery genre. Otaku print culture as a whole is beginning to obey a different kind of logic, one oriented toward characters rather than individual works. Seiryōin's novels, in fact, not only presuppose this as a condition but even satirize it. For example, in Japan Detective Club, 350 detectives are "divided into

Groups 1 through 7" and "during the Group Switch every two months the overachievers of a lower group are promoted while the under-achievers of a higher group are demoted without mercy."[37] This setting of the Japan Detective Club can be read as a parody of the whole situation, if one keeps in mind the character-oriented state of the market.

Neither literature nor entertainment, the otaku novels are already being sold and consumed according to a logic similar to that of video games and illustrations. Commercially speaking, the change from naturalist realism to "anime/manga-like realism" is sustained by this change in the market. As far as I know, Seiryōin is the author who reacted to this change most responsively and changed how he writes novels most fundamentally. Here, it is neither reality (naturalism) or an earlier fiction (narrative consumption) but the database of *moe*-elements that is felt as most real.

The Simulacra and the Database

Drawbacks of the Simulacra Theory

In the above discussion, otaku culture gives us an answer to the first of the two questions I asked at the beginning of this chapter: in post-modernity, how do simulacra increase? The surface outer layer of otaku culture is covered with simulacra, or derivative works. But in the deep inner layer lies the database of settings and characters, and further down, the database of *moe*-elements. The consumer behavior of the otaku, which might seem like a chaotic inundation of simulacra, becomes more ordered and understandable once we turn our eyes to the level of the database.

These observations, beyond an analysis of subculture, provide insights that would change the existing notion of the simulacra. In earlier theories on postmodernity, the increase in simulacra has been considered a chaotic phenomenon emerging after the demise of the distinction between the original and the copy. Such an argument cites, first and foremost, "The Work of Art in the Age of Mechanical Reproduction," a short essay written by Walter Benjamin more than sixty years ago. In it Benjamin famously argues that the sense of originality (called "aura") residing within a particular work of art is based upon the "singularity" of the "ritual" that gave birth to the work, but that the technology of mechanical reproduction voids such a sense.[38] This argument later became a core of simulacra theory.

Benjamin's grasp of "aura" here clearly reflects the aforementioned tree model. In front of an original, the viewer feels a connection with the "ritual" beyond the work at hand. There is no such connection with a copy. In other words, an original and a copy are distinguished by the presence of the connection with the ritual (i.e., the presence of the aura). This aesthetic indeed reflects a modern worldview. Figure 12 indicates this idea, based on Figure 3a. The omnipresence of simulacra represents a situation in which, having lost the very criteria for this connection, an original and a copy have come to have the same value and all signs have begun to float without their foundation.

Therefore, in the context of the earlier theories of postmodernity, the two phenomena I mentioned at the beginning of this chapter— "the omnipresence of simulacra" and "the decline of the grand narrative"—can in fact be grasped as two aspects of a single change: the collapse of the tree model. Of course, there is a fundamental difference between these two phenomena, in that the former is a change caused mainly by technological advances while the latter is a social, ideological change. Still, there is undeniably a common change in the worldview underlying these two phenomena. In fact, Benjamin's essay discusses the age of mechanical reproduction and the decline of ideologies as related phenomena, and Baudrillard grasps these two trends in relation to each other, arguing, "no more ideology, only simulacra."[39]

However, previous theories on postmodernity failed to understand that the tree model did not simply collapse but *was replaced by* the database model. Of course, some discussions have suggested such a point. For example, Baudrillard argues that, in contemporary society, permeated by marketing and semiotic consumption, "we live less as users than as readers and selectors, reading cells."[40] His argument that differentiated goods and signs are stocked and circulated in quantity (the totality of which Baudrillard calls "hyperreality") and that consumers can express their personality or originality only as a combination of them grasps a reality that very closely resembles what I have been calling the database model.

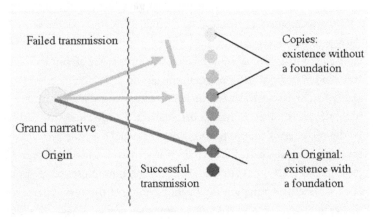

Figure 12. The original and the copy.

However, even in this discussion, the level of the simulacra and the level of the database have never been clearly distinguished, nor has the whole been grasped as a double-layer structure. Baudrillardian "hyperreality" covers both the world of the simulacra and the world of the database. In the example of otaku culture, the inundation of derivative works, narrative consumption, *chara-moe*, and even the so-called deformed designs such as Di Gi Charat would all be explained by the concept of "hyperreality."

From "Original versus Copy" to "Database versus Simulacra"

In contrast, in the present study I wish to show that the simulacra that are filling up this society have never propagated in a chaotic fashion but that their effective functioning is warranted first and foremost by the level of the database.

Otaku culture is filled with derivative works; originals and derivative works are produced and consumed as if they were of "equal value." However, not all of such derivative works actually have the same value; otherwise the market would not grow. In fact, underneath the simulacra exists a database, a device that sorts good simulacra from bad ones regulating the flow of derivative works. The 773rd Bikkuriman sticker must adequately share a common database with the previous

772 stickers, or it would not be regarded as a derivative work to begin with. *Ayanami Nurturing Project* must adequately share a worldview with *Evangelion,* and the design of Di Gi Charat must adequately sample *moe*-elements from the late 1990s. Simulacra created without recognition of these processes will be weeded out by the market and disappear.

In other words, in postmodernity, a new opposition is emerging between the simulacra and the database, in place of the previous opposition between the original and the copy. In the past, the original work was "an original" and the derivative work "a copy." Only herein exists the criterion for judging the quality of a work. For example, in the case of *Evangelion,* the TV series created by Anno Hideaki is a "work" connected with the authorship and his original message, while derivative works by amateurs and related commercial projects are mere copies. People are supposed to strictly distinguish between these two in consuming them.

However, in reality, over the past twenty years a consumer behavior that does not discriminate between these two categories has been gaining more and more power. Instead, as I mentioned above, the database of characters, settings, and *moe*-elements is on the rise and with it a different variety of standards applied to the database. On the rise instead are the database of character settings and *moe*-elements, as I have argued above, and emerging with it is a different kind of criteria based on one's relation to this database. A copy is judged not by its distance from an original but by its distance from the database. Figure 13 indicates this new relationship.

In contemporary thought, the magical attraction of the original as an original is sometimes called "the myth of authorship." As we survey the history of otaku culture from the 1980s to the 1990s to the 2000s, we find that even this myth has been rapidly declining. Most readers and experts in the field would agree that it is easy to name authors of major comics and anime that represent the 1980s, but it is more difficult to do the same for the 1990s. This observation might be seen as a symptom of the genre's decline, but in actuality, the very fact that it is difficult to name an author points to the essence of otaku culture in the 1990s. Now the author is no longer a god and therefore

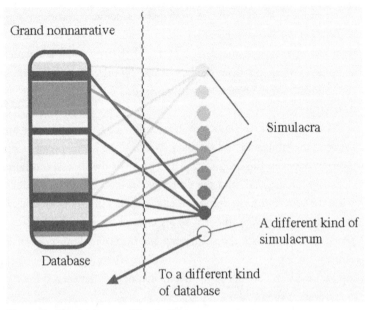

Grand nonnarrative

Simulacra

A different kind of
simulacrum

Database

To a different kind
of database

Figure 13. The database and the simulacra.

cannot be named. Instead, *moe*-elements have become gods. A moderately knowledgeable consumer should be able to name several major *moe*-elements representing the 1990s.

The Psychology of Derivative Works

The market for otaku culture consists of the double-layer structure of the simulacra and the database. Understanding this simple fact is important so as not to misunderstand the intentions of the otaku. For example, the inundation of simulacra, which is the reality of otaku culture, may seem radical and anarchistic from a certain viewpoint. But in fact the authors of derivative works do not exhibit such an aggressive intent. On the one hand they mercilessly parody, cut up, and remix the originals, but on the other hand they do not consider their actions to be a violation of the original works, and they stop their creative processes as soon as the original author asks them to do so. In this sense, they are rather conservative.

This duality may be incomprehensible at first, but it is easily understood through the aforementioned double-layer structure. As I have discussed repeatedly, the originals and the derivative works are both simulacra, and there is no fundamental difference between them.

Instead, the core of a work lies in the database of settings. Therefore, in the mind of the otaku, even if derivative works violate original works (at the level of the simulacra), the originality of the original works as information (at the level of the database) is protected and respected. Rather it is thought that, from the standpoint of authors of the derivative works, the increase of simulacra should raise the value of the originals. Of course, in reality the existence of the copyright should preclude such sensibility. However, more than a quarter century after the birth of the Comic Market, it is important to know the background of such psychology.

Discord between Murakami Takashi and the Otaku

Such a basic understanding would also be necessary when the fruits of otaku culture are brought beyond its bounds. The contemporary artist Murakami Takashi, whom I have mentioned several times, has endeavored most energetically to connect otaku culture to the outside world.

Born in 1962, Murakami would belong to the first generation of otaku and has even released many works influenced by anime and figurines, calling himself "an otaku who could not truly become one." His works, as seen in the DOB sequence (Figure 14) and the Second Mission Project Ko^2 sequence (Figure 15), are created both by focusing on the character designs that have been uniquely developed in otaku culture and by emphasizing, dissolving, and deforming their characteristics. I believe it is a great attempt to sublimate the oddities of the otaku simulacra into works of art,[41] but the otaku do not speak highly of them. On the contrary, Murakami's ventures have been criticized even by the otaku who have collaborated in his works.

One can name several reasons for this discord between Murakami and otaku, but among them are the structural characteristics of otaku culture as discussed above. Asano Masahiko, a creator of figurine molds

Figure 14. Takashi Murakami, *AND THEN Rainbow,* 2006. Acrylic on canvas mounted on board. 1000 x 1000 x 50 mm. Courtesy Galerie Emmanuel Perrotin, Paris and Miami. Copyright 2006 Murakami Takashi/Kaikai Kiki Co., Ltd. All rights reserved.

and one of the key figures in his role as editor for the production of Second Mission Project Ko^2, has said at an event that Murakami does not have "the otaku gene."[42] I think what he wanted to say is that Murakami lacks the ability to intuitively grasp various characteristics that make otaku works "otaku-like," i.e., the ability to grasp *moe*-elements.

In the world of contemporary art criticism, the production of simulacra is positioned as "a weapon that constitutes a new avant-garde."[43] And probably Murakami, too, was initially attracted to the surface layer of otaku culture as "avant-garde." Understood in this context, the DOB and the Second Mission Project Ko^2 are indeed works created by extracting and purifying the most radical and groundless parts

Figure 15. Takashi Murakami, *Second Mission Project Ko²* (ga-walk type), 1999. Oil paint, acrylic, synthetic resins, fiberglass, and iron. 2244 x 1769 x 1315 mm. Courtesy Blum & Poe. Copyright 1999 Murakami Takashi/Kaikai Kiki Co., Ltd. All rights reserved.

of the otaku designs, and in this sense they should be highly praised. For the otaku, however, this experiment by Murakami is nothing more than an incomplete attempt, extracting and imitating only the simulacra as designs (literally on the surface level) without understanding the database of *moe*-elements. Such a conceptual difference regarding the simulacra results in the different evaluation of Murakami's ventures by the contemporary art world and the otaku world.

Murakami's experiments, no matter how much they borrow the otaku designs, cannot be otaku-like in essence, insofar as they lack the level of the database. It is unclear how this affects the evaluation of Murakami as an artist, but it is useful to be cognizant of the difference between borrowing otaku designs and understanding the cultural structure behind such designs. However, in my opinion, Murakami's venture has been able to scrape out an aspect of otaku culture sharply *precisely because* he does not understand its structure, and that it is not a mere borrowing in this sense. Otaku designs at times have reached an extremely radical point, as the example of Di Gi Charat attests, but the authors themselves are often unaware of the designs' radicality because they are merely combinations of *moe*-elements for the authors. Murakami's works might be able to change this lack of awareness.

Snobbery and the Fictional Age

The Hegelian "End of History"

Let us proceed to the other question raised at the beginning of this book: If, in postmodernity, the notion of transcendence is in decline, what becomes of the humanity of human beings? To answer this question, first it is necessary to locate the meaning of the rise of the database consumption and the double-layer structure of postmodernity (discussed above) within a broad world historical view, one removed from discussion of a Japanese state of affairs.

In the first chapter I mentioned the philosopher Alexandre Kojève. Kojève was the Russian-born French philosopher who was famous for his unique 1930s lectures on Hegelian philosophy, which were published as *Introduction to the Reading of Hegel*.[44] In Hegelian philosophy, which was first developed in the early nineteenth century, the "Human" is defined as an existence with a self-consciousness, who, through a struggle with the "Other" (also endowed with self-consciousness), will move toward absolute knowledge, freedom, and civil society. Hegel called this process of struggle "History."

So Hegel claimed that history in this sense ended for Europe in the beginning of the nineteenth century. This claim may have seemed strange at first glance, but it is still very persuasive. This is because he declared that, when the modern society was about to be born, this very birth was "the end of history." There is a famous story that Hegel finished the manuscript of his magnum opus, *The Phenomenology of Spirit*, in Jena one day before Napoleon's invasion of the city. Of course, the mode of thought that sees the arrival of Western-style modern society as the conclusion of history has since been thoroughly criticized as being ethnocentric. However, looking at it another way, given that two centuries after Hegel was writing, modern values have covered the entire globe, this historical perspective is very difficult to refute.

The American "Return to Animality" and Japanese Snobbery

Regardless, what is important here is not Hegel's own thinking but the interpretation Kojève added to Hegel's philosophy of history. Specifically, it is a footnote added in the second edition of his *Introduction to the Reading of Hegel*, twenty years after the initial lectures, which became famous, at least in Japan. In the first chapter, in order to open simply, Kojève emphasizes that after the end of Hegelian history only two modes of existence remained for human beings. One was the pursuit of the American way of life, or what he called the "return to animality,"[45] and the other was Japanese snobbery.

Kojève called the form of consumer that arose in postwar America *animal*. His reason for using such a strong expression is related to the provisions for *humans* peculiar to Hegelian philosophy. According to Hegel (or more properly according to Kojève's interpretation of Hegel), Homo sapiens are not in and of themselves human. In order for human beings to be human, they must behave in a way that *negates* their own environment. To put it another way, they must struggle against nature.

Animals, in contrast, usually live in harmony with nature. Accordingly, postwar American consumer society—surrounded by products satisfying consumer "needs" alone and whose fashion changes accordion to the media's demands alone—is not, in his terminology, humanistic but, rather, "animalistic." Just as there is neither hunger nor strife, there is no philosophy: "After the end of History, men would construct their edifices and works of art as birds build their nests and spiders spin their webs, would perform musical concerts after the fashion of frogs and cicadas, would play like young animals, and would indulge in love like adult beasts," wrote Kojève with some frustration.[46]

On the other hand, *snobbery,* instead of having any essential reason for denying the given environment, is a behavioral pattern that denies being "based on formalized values." Snobs are not in harmony with their environment. Even if there is no chance whatsoever for denial, snobs presume to deny, to manufacture formal opposition, and to love the thrill of opposing nature. The example Kojève gives is ritual suicide *(seppuku).* In ritual suicide, in spite of having no reason to die, suicide is committed in essence because of the formal values of honor and order. This is the ultimate snobbery. This way of life is certainly not "animalistic" in that there are moments of negation. However, this also differs from the human way of life in the "historical" age. For the nature of snobs and their oppositional stance (for instance, the opposition to instinct at the time of ritual suicide) would no longer move history in any sense. No matter how many sacrificial corpses are piled up, ritual suicide, which is purely and courteously executed, certainly would not be a motivating force of revolution.

Japanese Snobbery Cultivated by Otaku Culture

Based only on a hunch and a short stay in Japan, the argument in Kojève's footnote consists largely of fantasies. However, when we look back at it, we can say that his prescient belief that the core of Japanese society is characterized by a mentality of snobbery, and that it will govern the cultural world, is frighteningly appropriate today.

To be sure, precisely after his pointing this out, otaku culture appeared in Japan and, proclaiming itself heir to Edo culture, cultivated a new snobbery. According to Okada Toshio's *Introduction to Otaku Studies,* to which we have already referred several times, otaku harbor a sense of distance best expressed in the following quip: "as they know they are being tricked, they can be truly emotionally moved." This has become a pillar of otaku sensibility. The otaku know that "it is quite meaningless to dare to watch 'childish' programs after becoming adults."[47] For example, the robot anime and squadron special effects dramas[48] that have deep-seated popularity with otaku expand on the

same kinds of narratives in the same kinds of settings, and to that extent an individual work can be said to have absolutely no meaning.
However, the otaku sensibility, according to Okada, consists in distinguishing values in form, "idea"[49] from this substantive meaninglessness.
This kind of detachment is precisely the characteristic of snobbery
described by Kojève.

For example, Kojève writes, "post-historical Man must continue to
detach 'form' from 'content,' doing so no longer in order to actively
transform the latter, but so that he may *oppose* himself as a pure 'form'
to himself and to others taken as a 'content' of any sort."[50] This kind
of description is extremely difficult to comprehend, but when we
compare it with the consumer behavior of the otaku pictured in *Introduction to Otaku Studies,* we can understand it in a very concrete way.

Posthistorical man, namely the otaku, is fully conversant with the
values and patterns of otaku works; he can consciously detach the
"idea" from them—which is to say, "to continue to *detach* 'form' from
'content.'" However, this detaching is no longer for the purpose of
finding meaning in various works or engaging in social activities but
rather is in order to confirm the self as a pure idle spectator (which is
"the self as pure form"). In this way, the otaku personify in some sense
the way of life in "posthistory" predicted fifty years ago by Kojève.
This means Okada's and Murakami's claims to see the future of the
world in otaku also contain a certain kind of truth.

The Twentieth Century Ruled by Cynicism

The attitude toward the world that Kojève called snobbery was further theorized in detail and called *cynicism* by the Slovenian-born
scholar of psychoanalysis Slavoj Žižek. As an example of cynicism, he
repeatedly cited Cold War Stalinism. In his *Sublime Object of Ideology,*
published in 1989, he wrote:

> To exemplify this connection (the relationship between Hegelian phi-
> losophy and Lacanian psychoanalysis) let us refer to Stalinism—more
> specifically, to its obsessive insistence that whatever the cost we must
> *maintain the appearance:* we all know that behind the scenes there are
> wild factional struggles going on; nevertheless we must keep at any

price the appearance of Party unity; nobody really believes in the ruling ideology, every individual preserves a cynical distance from it and
everybody knows that nobody believes in it; but still, the appearance is
to be maintained at any price that people are enthusiastically building
socialism, supporting the party, and so on.... We could thus say that
Stalinism has a value as the ontological proof of the existence of the
big Other.[51]

Supporters of Stalinism actually know that it is a lie. However, *precisely because of* this, they cannot stop appearing to believe in it. This
twisted relationship between form and substance is identical to the
attitude called "snobbery" by Kojève. Snobbish, cynical subjects do
not believe in the material value of the world. However, it is exactly
because of this that they cannot stop appearing to believe in the formal value of the world; so they do not mind sacrificing substance for
appearance or form. Kojève grasped this "precisely because of" as an
activity of the subject. But Žižek argues that this reversal is a compul-
sory mechanism that the subject can do nothing about. Even knowing
it to be a lie, people believe in Stalinism; even knowing it is meaningless, people commit seppuku. Even though it is disagreeable, it cannot
be stopped.

According to Žižek's theory, this paradox is related to the principles
of human psychology. Consequently, when we read his work, it is as if
the reversal found in his words "precisely because of" is confirmed
from Greek philosophy through Hitchcock to Coca-Cola in every
time and place.

However, I think this kind of universality is a bit doubtful. There
is not space here to write in detail the reasons for this, so I want to
give attention to only one: the fact that the theory of cynicism in *The
Sublime Object of Ideology* was built on the *Critique of Cynical Reason*
by German critic Peter Sloterdijk, originally published in 1983. The
cynicism Sloterdijk examines is entirely a phenomenon of the twentieth century. He writes the following:

> The First World War signals the turning point in modern cynicism.
> With it the up-tempo phase of the decomposition of old naïvetés be-
> gins—such as those about the nature of war, the nature of social order,

of progress, of bourgeois values, indeed of bourgeois civilization itself. Since this war, the diffuse schizoid climate around the major European powers has not become any less intense.... Everything positive will be from then on an "In-spite-of," laced with latent desperation.[52]

The experience of World War I and the subsequent ruination of Europe thoroughly devastated the nineteenth-century trust in enlightenment and reason. My idea is that Žižek's theory of cynicism, contrary to what he himself asserts, is not a universal principle of humanity; rather, it is subtly set up as an analysis of a "twentieth-century mentality" that was born in the outcome of this war. This is naturally true, in a sense, because the theories of the French psychoanalyst Jacques Lacan, to which Žižek frequently refers, were themselves derived from the same experience of the Great War. For instance, Lacan paid close attention to the work of Freud's later years (such as those pieces dealing with the death wish and the repetition compulsion), but that work was indeed written from the middle of World War I through the postwar years. Furthermore, in addition to Freudian theory, the philosophy of Heidegger and the surrealist movement, both of which influenced Lacan, were born in the same period. Accordingly, the previously mentioned analysis by Žižek can be seen as an attempt to explain the realities (that is, the ideology of the Cold War) and theories (Lacan) that were both hatched out of World War I. I am sorry I cannot go into this in a more concrete way here, but Žižek's various cultural and social critiques are extremely sophisticated, if we gain a certain distance from them. In his work, most phenomena are explained through a reverse cynicism, but actually that is the reflection of our society, which truly has been ruled by cynicism during the past century.

As I explained in the beginning of this chapter, postmodernity refers to the conditions of the cultural world since the 1970s. However, taking a broader perspective, we can go back as far as the 1920s and 1930s to find the budding of postmodernity in the appearance of new technologies of reproduction, the origins of information theory, and even changing views of human beings. The aforementioned Benjamin essay was written in 1936, and it was World War I more than anything else that first began the decline of "grand narratives" such as

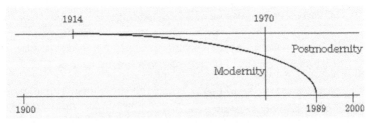

Figure 16. The transition from modernity to postmodernity.

"reason" and "enlightenment." And, conversely, it was only in 1989 that this decline was finally brought to the surface, when, with the end of the Cold War, the ghost of the last grand narrative, called "communism," finally disappeared. Consequently, the shift from modernity to postmodernity can be thought of as something gradually occurring over the seventy-five years between 1914 and 1989, with a single focus in the 1970s (see Figure 16).

I think Žižek is the thinker who theorized that structure in the most easily understandable way and who most beautifully reflected the spirit of the transitional period. To sum up the twentieth century, we might say it was characterized already by the loss of a transcendental grand narrative, as is well known—but one had to believe in the semblance of a grand narrative, and furthermore, *the semblance that life is meaningful.* To put it another way, the twentieth century was partially postmodern. Today the paradox that "life has no meaning; but because life has no meaning, we live" has lost its importance. But this way of thinking must have held extreme urgency during the Cold War period.

Cynicism Found in Otaku Snobbery

From this point of view, otaku snobbery appears to be a manifestation of the worldwide trend toward cynicism, as well as an extension of the formalism of Edo culture. Since the political stresses and social conditions of Japanese otaku certainly differed from those of Soviet citizens under Stalinism, comparing them may seem like a joke. But they do have in common the mental process that, after relativizing the value of everything, brazenly finds meaning in the meaningless and then at some point finds that "brazenness" itself inescapable. This is precisely how Kojève, without really knowing much about Japan, could foresee the rise of an otaku sensibility.

Among the past theories on otaku, Ōsawa Masachi himself has mentioned this point. As I have described, he sought a characteristic of otaku in the substitution of subculture for the fallen grand narrative (the agency of the transcendent other). It is at this point that he refers to Žižek and develops a theory of otaku that completely corresponds with the above theory of cynicism. Ōsawa notes that there is "the secondary projection of the agency of the third party, under the assumption of the primary collapse of the agency of the third party"; at that point he emphasizes that these projections are "desperate measures" for the otaku to live in today's society.[53] Although Ōsawa's terminology is unique, if we put his expressions into the terminology of this book the "agency of the third party" is the transcendental other, or the grand narrative; and the "secondary projection" is a fabrication by subculture. After the collapse of the authentic and primary grand narrative, the otaku built a fake grand narrative (a secondary projection) under this assumption. They cannot relinquish that fake.

The Idealistic Age and the Fictional Age

Beyond this assumption, Ōsawa makes even deeper critical observations in works such as *The End of the Fictional Age* and *Postwar Intellectual Space*.[54] According to Ōsawa, the ideological circumstances of postwar Japan can be divided into two periods—*the idealistic age* from 1945 to 1970 and *the fictional age* from 1970 to 1995. To render it in my own terms, the "idealistic age" is the period when grand narrative functioned alone while the "fictional age" is the period when grand narrative functioned only as a fake. In this framework, otaku narrative consumption—emphasizing fiction—can be grasped as "a thorough form of a consumer society's cynicism" in the context of a consistent trend from the end of the war through the 1980s. So the Aum Shinrikyō incident of 1995 is truly positioned as the end of that trend. "If the Red Army and the people who sensed themselves to be of that same period represent the demise (or limits) of the idealistic age, Aum Shinrikyō represents the demise (or limits) of the fictional age."[55]

The seventy-five years from 1914 to 1989 was a long transitional period from the modernity of the nineteenth century to the postmodernity of the twenty-first century. The mindset of the transitional age was characterized by cynicism or snobbery that peaked in the Cold War era. However, in Japan, this process was severed at once by the defeat of 1945. Conversely, from postwar reconstruction to the period of high growth, Japan surmounted danger by restoring grand narratives (i.e., national goals/interests) and by strengthening the social ideological apparatuses such as educational facilities and social organizations.[56] In reality, the efficient economic growth of this period was supported largely by the administrative and legal systems left behind by the structures of total war set up during World War II. This synthesis was once again relaxed in the 1970s. The result for Japan was that the transition to postmodernity began in earnest in the 1970s, but at a much quicker pace. The reason the opposition between Ōsawa's "idealistic age" and "fictional age" is clear is probably because it is based on a situation peculiar to the history of Japan.

The Dissociated Human

Rising Desire for a Well-constructed Narrative

As Ōsawa emphasizes, we no longer live in the "fictional age." The spirit of cynicism/snobbery has lost its validity both globally and in Japan, and a new model for subject formation is emerging. Within this larger perspective, the transition from narrative consumption to database consumption is not simply a shift within the subculture but reflects a much larger movement. What kind of model can be glimpsed behind database consumption?

What is noteworthy in this regard is that, within otaku culture, there is an increasing interest in the drama within a work, coinciding with the decline of the grand narrative. So far I have argued that no grand narrative is needed in otaku culture. But in fact, as we can see in the novelization boom and the revived interest in narratives within comics since *Evangelion*, there seems to be a rising desire for a well-constructed narrative that holds readers' (or viewers') attention for a while, emotionally moves them a little, and makes them think a little. In my opinion, this contradiction most clearly reveals the nature of subjectivity as an agent of database consumption.

The "Games for Reading" at the Center of Otaku Culture

Let us consider specific examples. In otaku culture of the 1990s, PC games called "girl games" or "beautiful girls games" play a significant role. This game genre was first created in 1982, proliferated in the early 1990s, and reached its peak in the late 1990s.[57] "Girl games" are basically adult-only games, played not on consumer game consoles (such as NES/"FamiCom" or Sony PlayStation) but mainly on Windows machines. Their basic format is quite simple: the player tries to "win over" female characters of their choice through various game systems, and, if successful, they can view pornographic illustrations as a reward. This very simplicity, however, has generated several intriguing experiments.

Among such forays, I wish to focus here on "novel games," a subgenre of girl games that, at the center of otaku culture since *Evangelion*, has sustained the prosperity of the girl games in the late 1990s and generated numerous derivative works and related goods.

In general, novel games are multistory, multiending novels (which in the past were rendered as "gamebooks") that can be "read" on the computer screen with images and sounds. The basic interface is easily understood if you can imagine a picture scroll or a *kamishibai*, picture-story show. This game system was first established in *Hypericum (Otogirisō)* on Super Nintendo but was introduced to the world of girl games in 1996 with *Droplet*. *Droplet* was produced by Leaf, a production company run by second-generation otaku, and with its sequels *The Scar* and *To Heart (Tō Hāto)* the game still boasts cult-like popularity.

Basically, all that the player of a novel game does is to read the texts and choose from the given options. The degree of freedom is much lower than that of action games and role-playing games, and there is little room for taking advantage of animation and real-time 3-D graphics. For this reason, the technological advancement of consumer game consoles had a negative effect on the novel games, but in the low-budget adult PC game industry, this paucity of features worked in its favor. From this point on, "novel games" refers to those in the latter group, i.e., the novel games as girl games, unless otherwise noted. In any case, in recent years many of the novel games released for consumer game consoles were rereleases of the PC girl games.

The player of novel games, unlike players of other kinds of games, is overwhelmingly passive. For most of the playing time, the player simply reads texts and views illustrations. It is true that, in recent years, many games use animations and rich background music as well as feature well-known voice actors and actresses, and there are some quite intriguing experiments among them. Still, texts and illustrations continue to constitute the main features of novel games. Until only a few years ago, it was difficult for personal computers to process voices and animation because they are data-intensive, so the novel games could not use them even if their creators had wanted to. Due to this restriction, the development of novel games almost necessarily concentrated on the pursuit of texts that could effectively trigger emotion (ones over which one can cry) and illustrations for which one can feel a strong empathy (or feel *moe*). The multistory, multiending structure pushed this tendency further. The multiple stories and multiple endings (i.e., multiple women to "win over") required combining as many stories and as many characters as possible through efficient combination of the necessary modules.

Developed with a low budget and for rudimentary hardware, novel games were adult-only games stripped of unnecessary literary or artistic flair. For the reasons mentioned above, they have developed into a unique genre that most efficiently reflects the otaku's passion toward *moe*-elements. Therefore, the role that the novel games have played in otaku culture in the past several years is enormous. For example, after *Evangelion* the most influential character among the male otaku is not a character in anime or comics but probably "Multi" in *To Heart* (Figure 17).

Figure 17. "Multi HMX-12." In *To Heart Visual Fan Book* (Tokyo: Digital Works, 1999), 125.

What It Means "To Be Able to Cry" over Novel Games

In this way, the novel-games genre reveals especially strongly the characteristics of database consumption, even within contemporary otaku culture largely dominated by this database consumption. As a result, some of these games have even lost original characteristics of girl games and instead create a unique world with more emphasis on the combination of *moe*-elements rather than pornographic elements. Typical examples of this are *Kanon* (1999) and *Air* (2000), both produced by Key (Figure 18).

Although both of these works are categorized for adult-only sales, they now contain hardly any pornographic illustrations. Games produced by Key are designed not to give erotic satisfaction to consumers but to provide an ideal vehicle for otaku to efficiently cry and feel *moe*, by a thorough combination of the *moe*-elements popular among otaku. For example, in *Air*, pornographic illustrations of all sorts are concentrated in the first half, as if to reject the premise that the goal of girl games is erotic satisfaction. The latter half of the ten-plus hours of playing time does not even contain substantial choices; the player only follows the texts as a melodrama unfolds about a heroine. Even this melodrama is rather typical and abstract, created out of a combination of *moe*-elements such as "incurable disease," "fate from previous lives," and "a lonely girl without a friend." The story of *Air* moves on as a barebones structure of combined settings, while leaving important questions unanswered, such as where the story takes place, what the heroine's illness is, or in what age "the past lives" were.

Nevertheless, this kind of game is a great commercial success— selling more than one hundred thousand copies despite its high price— because, like the successful strategy of *Di Gi Charat*, it masterfully grasps all of the fundamentals of *moe*, from the types of narrative to the details of design. As I mentioned with regard to novels by Seiryōin Ryūsui, the *moe*-elements extracted from the subculture database seem far more real than the imitation of the real world for the emergent group of consumers in the 1990s.

Therefore, in most cases when they say "it's deep" or they "can cry," the otaku are merely making a judgment on the excellence in the

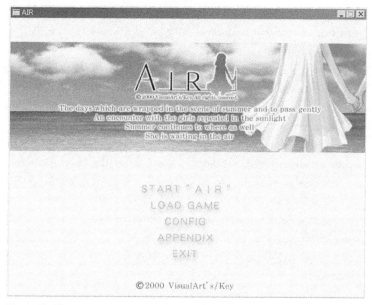

The days which are wrapped in the scene of summer and to pass gently
An encounter with the girls repeated in the sunlight
Summer continues to where as well
She is waiting in the air

START " A I R "
LOAD GAME
CONFIG
APPENDIX
EXIT

© 2000 VisualArt's/Key

Figure 18. The startup screen for *Air.* Produced by Key.

combination of *moe*-elements. In this sense, the rising interest in drama that occurred in the 1990s is not essentially different from the rising interest in cat ears and maid costumes. What is sought here is not the narrative dynamism of old, but a formula, without a worldview or a message, that effectively manipulates emotion.

Toward the Possibility of Producing a More Thorough Simulacrum

There is yet another aspect to the consumption of novel games. Unlike novels and comics, the substance of computer games is sought not in the drama that the player sees on the screen (a small narrative) but in the system that generates such a drama. Whether in action games or role-playing games, the images on the screen or the narrative development are but one possible version generated according to the player's keystrokes. If the player plays differently, the same game can display a different set of screens or narrative development. And the consumer of the games as a matter of course receives not only the single story at hand but also the sum of different versions of *possible stories.* Therefore, an analysis of novel games must pay attention to this double-layer structure in order to avoid the mistake of employing a framework from literary or film criticism.

Clearly, this structure reflects the postmodern world image (the database model) that we have analyzed thus far. Therefore, there is a deep relationship between the development of computer games and the development of postmodernity; this relationship is obvious just from the temporal coincidence, but I will discuss this point on another occasion. Here it suffices to say that for the novel game, as a kind of computer game, the user's attitude toward it is double-layered as well. As mentioned above, the consumption of novel games at the outer surface layer satisfies with combinations of *moe*-elements, and the otaku fully enjoy the indulgence of crying and *moe*. This is definitely true, but when we look more closely, another kind of desire can be discerned.

More concretely, there is a desire to invade the system of a novel game itself and to extract the raw information *before* it is constituted on a playing screenshot, and to reconstitute an entirely different work with the material. Many screenshots of novel games are constructed from a combination of multiple data. The three images on the right of Figure 19 are screenshots from *The Scar,* but they can all be resolved into various electronic files, as indicated on the left of the figure. For example, the screenshot on the top right was created by overlaying the image of the character (in the system designated by the file name "C31.LFG") on the background image of a Japanese-style room ("S10.LFG") and laying the texts of the scenario (part of the file designated as "016.SCN") over them. In addition, as indicated in the figure, the same texts and images can generate various screenshots depending on combinations. The recycling of files is desirable by necessity, not only because of the streamlining of the production process but also because of hardware conditions (limits on the capacity of recording media).

Such recycling of images is by no means uncommon and is often seen in comics and anime. In anime in particular, most screens consist of multiple overlapping cells, and the idea is not that different with the novel games. One crucial difference between novel games and

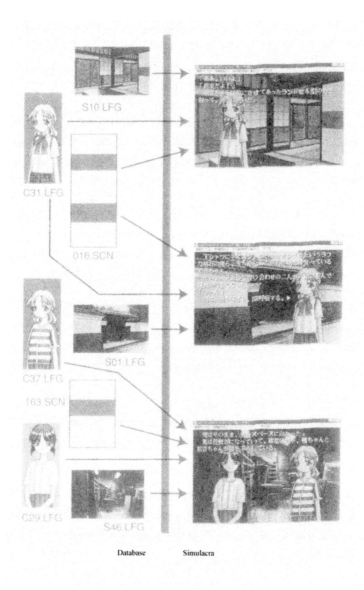

Database   Simulacra

Figure 19. Double-layered structure of novel games.

anime, however, is that in novel games fragments of the screen are not only used by producers but can also be easily analyzed and made into a database by consumers. The text and image files as indicated in the figure are often unreadable at the time of purchase, because they are actually compressed and encrypted. However, many consumers of girl games are computer users who have abundant technical knowledge and have the hacker's mentality. As a result, on the Internet there is freeware that analyzes the data and "extracts" scenarios, images, and sounds from the data of such major games as *The Scar*. I used one such freeware application in order to create the figure here.[58]

Such an environment pushes the derivative works in novel games a step further than before. As I explain above, derivative works are works presented as simulacra, which are created as a combination of arbitrarily chosen fragments in the database extracted from the settings of the original. However, in the derivative works of the past, the database utilized is an abstract one, reconstructed independently by the consumers, and this leaves room for the originality of the author. For example, the authors of the fanzines of *Evangelion* dissolved the original into fragments and reassembled them, but they had to draw the actual pages of the fanzines by themselves; some kind of authorship resides there. There were some attempts to create derivative works by sampling the TV series (those were called "mad video"), but in part due to the technological limitations of the time, it did not become a major movement.

But in the latter half of the 1990s, the rise of the novel games, the popularization of analysis described above, and the enrichment of multimedia environment to reconstitute the data enabled the production of more thorough simulacra that are qualitatively different from those derivative works. One example of this is a type of video work called a "mad movie." This is a short video clip created by capturing the screens of anime and games and manipulating and editing them to some music, and is mainly circulated over the Internet. One difference from the what used to be called the "mad video" in the 1980s is that the entire editing process has been digitized, and as a result the intentions and the motives of the producers become quite different.

In particular, the works created as derivative works of novel games have made quite unique developments.

For example, among the mad movies of *Air* are works created by using the images extracted from *Air* almost untouched, edited with the music extracted from the game. Here, unlike the derivative works in fanzines, a new type of derivative work is emerging that uses the exact same data as the original but is created by changing the combinations and modes of expression. Recently, there have been many interesting examples along these lines, such as an attempt to create a completely different game using the same character images and voice data, or an attempt to independently transplant a Windows version of a novel game to another operating system.

These new types of derivative works are much more likely to cause copyright issues than the previous types such as fanzines, because they use the original data as is. Creators seem to be aware of this problem, and some of these attempts are exchanged over the Internet for only a limited time. I am not in the position to comment on the present state of creating derivative works out of the actual data taken from the original, but I wish to draw the reader's attention to the fact that such a desire to create derivative works in this way is not an individual aberration but a desire necessarily born out of the essence of the novel games (and, ultimately, the essence of postmodernity).

As I said earlier, a scene in a novel game, even in the original, is created by combining multiple data. A screen and a plot, which seem unitary on the surface outer layer, are just an aggregate of meaningless fragments in the deep inner layer. There, the same texts and images are given several different roles, according to the operation of the player. If so, it is a natural development to think that, in reverse, one might create a *different version* (but as valuable as the original) of the novel game by combining these fragments differently. Creators of mad movies are enthusiastically analyzing the system and recombining the data in order to realize again the same emotional experience that they experienced with the original, but in a different combination. At least in their minds, this activity is led by a consciousness fundamentally different from plagiarism, parodying, and sampling.

The Disparate Coexistence of Small Narratives
and Grand Nonnarrative

In this way, the consumers of novel games can be characterized as having two completely different inclinations toward the surface outer layer (the drama) and toward the deep inner layer (the system) of a work. In the former they look for an effective emotional satisfaction through combinations of *moe*-elements. In contrast, in the latter they want to dissolve the very unit of the work that gives them such satisfaction, reduce it to a database, and create new simulacra. In other words, in otaku the desire for small narratives and the desire for database coexist separately from each other.

In my opinion, this indicates, through the structure of cultural consumption, a mode of subjectivity in an age when snobbery and fiction have come to an end and the database model has become dominant. Modern individuals traced a path back from small narratives to a grand narrative; individuals at the transition from modernity to postmodernity needed snobbism in order to bridge the gap between them. However, postmodern individuals let the two levels, small narratives and a grand nonnarrative, coexist separately without necessarily connecting them. To put it more clearly, they learn the technique of living without connecting the deeply emotional experience of a work (a small narrative) to a worldview (a grand narrative). Borrowing from psychoanalysis, I call this schism *dissociative*.

Interestingly, many novel games tend to reinforce this sense of dissociation intentionally at the level of the content. As mentioned above, novel games presuppose multiple stories and endings. Therefore, the player cannot pursue a relationship with only one woman. The very structure of novel games essentially requires the player to wander from relationship to relationship. Nevertheless, in a scenario for a novel game, the protagonist (the object of the player's identification) is rarely defined as a debaucher, switching from one girlfriend to another. Instead, "destiny" and "pure love" with the heroine are emphasized. Therefore such a game embraces a clear contradiction: although the protagonist is depicted as someone who experiences pure love at each juncture and encounters his "woman of destiny," actually each of the different encounters that results from the player's choices is called "destiny." Here, there is a vast discrepancy between the drama required by the characteristics of the system and the drama prepared in each scene.

However, at the current phase of database consumption, this contradiction is not felt as a contradiction. At the level of the deep inner layer of the work (i.e., the database), there exist several different destinies (junctures) for the protagonist. However, at the surface outer layer of the work, i.e., at the level of the drama, there is only one destiny for the protagonist, and the player identifies with, feels empathy for, and is sometimes emotionally moved by it. The players of novel games do not feel this as a contradiction. While they realize that there are several different destinies within the work, they emotionally relate to the world of the work as if the randomly selected choice before them at a given moment is the only destiny.

The reader might perhaps find it difficult to understand a dissociated mental process such as this. In the modern novel, behind the protagonist's small narrative was always a grand narrative that gave it meaning. Therefore, there was only one ending to the novel and that ending could never be changed.

In the postmodern novel games, by contrast, the protagonist's small narrative will never be given meaning by a grand narrative. Each narrative is nothing more than a simulacrum constituted by a combination of randomly chosen finite elements extracted from the database. They can be reproduced again and again at will, and yet from a different point of view the narratives are a "destiny" that cannot be reproduced in the sense that a cast of a die is random and preordained at the same time. Whether you think that the meaning given by a grand narrative is destiny or you think it is the scarcity of the combinations selected from the bundle of finite possibilities that is destiny, I doubt that the importance of this stops with the differences between novels and novel games but rather symbolically reveals the differences between modern and postmodern life skills. Although I can only analyze otaku culture in this book, I think that more broadly this dissociative coexistence of *the desire for a small narrative* at the level of simulacra and *the desire for a grand nonnarrative* at the level of database is a structure that generally characterizes subjectivity in postmodern society.

The Animal Age

A Society Sufficient without the Other

According to Kojève, after the loss of the grand narrative only two choices remain—animality and snobbery. Thus far, this book has argued that the role of snobbery as a zeitgeist ended in 1989 for the world (and for Japan in 1995) and that now a different zeitgeist is evolving, moving toward database consumption. Based on Kojève's rhetoric, I think it fitting to place the name *animalization* on that transition.

What is animalization? Kojève's *Introduction to the Reading of Hegel* has a unique definition of the difference between the human and the animal. Key to this definition is the difference between desire and need.[59] According to Kojève, humans have desire, as opposed to animals, which have only needs. The word *need* indicates a simple craving or thirst that is satisfied through its relationship with a specific object. For example, animals sensing hunger will be completely satisfied by eating food. This circuit between lack and satisfaction is the defining characteristic of need. Even human life is strongly driven by such needs.

However, humans have a distinct species of craving—*desire*. Different from need, desire does not disappear when the object of desire is obtained and the lack is satisfied. For Kojève and French thinkers influenced by him, a favorite example of this variety of craving is the male's sexual desire for the female. The male desire for the female does not end even when the male obtains a partner's body, but rather swells more and more (according to Kojève and others). This is because sexual desire is not a simple thing satisfied with a sense of physiological climax; rather it has a complex structure, wherein *the desire of the other is itself desired.* Simply put, even after a man gets a woman, in reality he wants that fact to be desired by (excite the jealousy of) the other. Or, at the same time, he thinks he wants to get that which the other desires (is jealous of), so that desire is never exhausted. Humans differ from animals in their self-consciousness; the reason they can build social relations is because they have intersubjective desire. Animal needs can be satisfied without the other, but for human desires the other is essentially necessary; and here I will not go into detail, but this distinction is an extremely grand premise that is the basis for modern philosophy and thought from Hegel to Lacan. And Kojève, too, maintains this.

Consequently, "becoming animal" means the erasure of this kind of intersubjective structure and the arrival of a situation in which each person closes various lack–satisfaction circuits. What Kojève labeled "animalistic" was the postwar, American-style consumer society. But, based on this context, we can still find in that word a sharp insight that is more than a simple impression.

The logic of American-style consumer society has grown steadily since the 1950s and has now spread throughout the world. Today's consumer society has been standardized, media-ized, and it has developed a meticulously well-kept distribution management system. In it, improvements accumulate day after day so that consumer needs are satisfied immediately and mechanically, without the intervention of the other. The objects of desire that previously could not be had without social communication, such as everyday meals and sexual partners, can now be obtained very easily, without all that troublesome communication, through fast food or the sex industry. So it can be said that in this way our society has truly been stepping down the path of animalization for several decades. As previously mentioned, Kojève predicted that in this society the world would become a place where people "would perform musical concerts after the fashion of frogs and cicadas, would play like young animals, and would indulge in love like adult beasts."[60] If we look at today's mature, computerized consumer society, we can see that Kojève's prediction has been nearly realized.

The "Animalistic" Consuming Behavior of the Otaku

In this perspective, the adjective "animalistic" is indeed appropriate for the otaku consuming behavior, positing *moe* for *Di Gi Charat*, reading Seiryōin Ryūsui's *Cosmic*, and crying over the girl game *Air*. As we see again and again, snobbery is no longer necessary for the otaku of today. The desire for a grand narrative that gave birth to snobbery is itself now weakening. Instead, demanding the right formula of *moe*-elements that more effectively realizes emotional satisfaction, they consume and cull new works one after another.

Accordingly, if otaku discover some new element, most characters and narratives are immediately transformed, and from the assembled and negotiated permutations of multiple elements many analogous works are born. Within the collective and anonymous works in aggregate, traditional authorship plays an extremely small role. The intensity of the works does not come from the message or narrative embedded there by the author but is decided according to the compatible preferences of consumers and the *moe*-elements dispersed in the works.

So if we were to stretch our chain of association, this sort of otaku behavioral principle can be thought of as differing from that of intellectual aficionados (conscious people), whose interest is based in cool judgment, and from that of fetishistically indulgent sexual subjects (unconscious people). But rather, more simply and directly, the otaku behavioral principle can be seen as close to the behavioral principle of drug addicts. Not a few otaku tell a heartfelt story that, having once encountered some character designs or the voices of some voice actors, that picture or voice circulates through that otaku's head as if the neural wiring had completely changed. This resembles a drug dependency rather than a hobby.

The Conservative Sexuality of the Otaku

Actually, there are some cases that can be better explained by taking this kind of confession of personal experience at face value. Psychiatrist Saitō Tamaki raises the following question in several occasions: Why are there very few actual perverts amongst otaku, even though the icons of otaku culture are filled with all sorts of sexual perversions?[61] Since the 1980s, much has been made about male otaku possessing pictures of Lolitas and female otaku enjoying the "yaoi" genre featuring male homosexuals;[62] on the other hand, everyone knows that among the otaku there are not so many real pedophiles or homosexuals. Accordingly, Saitō's raising of this question should be of profound interest.

Unfortunately, Saitō's answer is too complex. According to his explanation, the otaku have lost a grand narrative (in Saitō's terms they've "failed in their symbolic castration"), and in order to fill the loss they need to sever real sexuality from imaginary sexuality and supplement the loss of the former with the latter. As a result, their creations are filled with excessively sexual images. This analysis probably highlights a certain aspect of otaku psychology, but, as far as explaining the phenomena concerned, Saitō's logic is unnecessarily circumlocutory.

With the continuing trend toward animalization in mind, there is a much more simple explanation of the same reality. Just as animal needs and human desires differ, so do genital needs and subjective "sexuality" differ. Many of the otaku today who consume adult comics and "girl games" probably separate these two; and their genitals simply and animalistically grew accustomed to being stimulated by perverted images. Since they were teenagers, they had been exposed to innumerable otaku sexual expressions: at some point, they were trained to be sexually stimulated by looking at illustrations of girls, cat ears, and maid outfits. However, anyone can grasp that kind of stimulation if they are similarly trained, since it is essentially a matter of nerves. In contrast, it takes an entirely different motive and opportunity to undertake pedophilia, homosexuality, or a fetish for particular attire as one's own sexuality. In most cases, the sexual awareness of the otaku does not reach that level in any way.[63] Precisely because of this, otaku have a strange Janus-faced quality (just as in the previously mentioned case of their attitude toward derivative works): on the one hand, they consume numerous perverse images, while on the other hand, they are surprisingly conservative toward actual perversion.

From the Fictional Age to the Animal Age

The massive trend from the fabrication of grand narratives to their simple disposal, from *Gundam* to *Di Gi Charat*, from narrative consumption to database consumption, that is to say *from the partial postmodern to the total postmodern* means the animalization of people living in the animal age. Consequently, here I build on and continue the discussion of Ōsawa Masachi, which considers 1945 to 1970 as the

idealistic age and 1970 to 1995 as the fictional age, by calling the period from 1995 *the animal age.* As I've said repeatedly, this transformation, or the animalization of consumers, was born out of global
postmodernization and was by no means a solely domestic phenomenon. Moreover, just as the opposition between the idealistic age and
the fictional age is acute, it is clear that the movement from the fictional age to the animal age, too, was particularly fast in Japan.

Here it is instructive to look at the behavioral pattern of the so-
called *kogal*[64]—the street girls on whom 1990s journalism foraged as
much as it did on otaku, though in different ways. As I don't know
much about this tendency, my consideration will have to rely on general
mass media coverage, and I can only give some rough impressions.
However, within those bounds, the *kogal* behavioral pattern, though it
possesses many traits that appear on the surface to be the polar opposite of the otaku, of course can still be thought of as "animalistic." The
girls hardly resisted selling their own sexual bodies, an act which they
separate from their consciously chosen modes of sexuality; engaging
in essentially isolated communication despite having many acquain-
tances, they choose to lead a lifestyle extremely sensitive to the satisfaction of their needs.

Similarities between the *Kogal* and the Otaku

The emergence of the *kogal* is not at all unrelated to the changes in
otaku culture. In the late 1990s, the sociologist Miyadai Shinji became famous as an expert in the culture of the street girls, and the
trajectory of his problematic was quite close to that of Ōtsuka Eiji
and Ōsawa Masachi, and all three belong to the same generation. By
tracing his writings, it becomes quite clear that the two subcultures,
i.e., the otaku and the *kogal,* emerged as a reflection of the same social
transformation.

For example, *The Choice of the School Uniform Girls,* the book in
which Miyadai took up the *kogal* (then known as the "bloomer and
sailor suit girls") as the main theme for the first time, is also noteworthy for its excellent discussion on the otaku in its latter half.[65] According to Miyadai, since 1973 the sense of community within a generation has been lost in Japanese society, and youth groups became

"island universes." In the 1980s, the people known as "new Homo sapiens"[66] and "the otaku" were the first groups to adjust to this change. Miyadai characterizes the principles of action for the "new Homo sapiens" and the otaku as "depthless communication based on the symbolic exchanges and a self-image that is barely maintained within the limited information space"; they emphasize fictional, symbolic exchanges "in order to artificially make up for the presuppositions of communication that have become weaker than before."[67] Clearly, this analysis points to the same psychological process that Ōtsuka called "narrative consumption" and Ōsawa called "the secondary projection of the agency of the third party." This desire to fabricate a replacement for the lost grand narrative out of subculture is what Miyadai calls "a global meaning-giving strategy."

However, as *The Choice of the School Uniform Girls* emphasizes, in the 1990s this very strategy had become saturated, making it difficult to maintain even "the limited information space." In our terminology, it is the age in which even narrative consumption has become difficult. Based on this understanding, in 1995 Miyadai greatly appreciated practical action principles among the street girls and began journalistic activities with the slogans such as "Taking-it-easy *[mattari]* Revolution" and "From Meaning to Intensity." It is difficult to provide specific quotes of Miyadai from this period, as he failed to give a sustained argument; but his basic attitude is quite obvious from these slogans and various essays he wrote. There are curious coincidences between this and the questions of database consumption discussed thus far.

For example, in *Live the Endless Everyday,* which is a collection of Miyadai's essays published immediately following the Aum Shinrikyō sarin gas attack on the Tokyo subway in 1995, he persistently discusses the contrast between "those who cannot adjust to the endless everyday" and "those who can adjust to it." Members of the Aum Shinrikyō cult represent the former, while the "bloomer and sailor suit girls" fall into the latter. Given this contrast, Miyadai writes that it is probably possible to resolve the insularity of the former intellectually, but "such an approach is so mesmerizingly circuitous that one must wonder if it could ever be an effective strategy." Miyadai goes on to say: "but I believe that there is another, completely different path:

it is to abandon a total, comprehensive demand. It is a decisive path that we have already begun to take."[68] In a highly encoded and anonymous city culture, the "bloomer and sailor suit girls" of the 1990s adopted a take-it-easy attitude "without telling Yumi from Yuka"; for them, there is neither the will to capture the entire world in their perspectives ("a total, comprehensive answer") nor the excessive self-consciousness caused by abandoning such will. They do not have a "meaning-giving strategy" nor do they need narrative consumption.

This is the very "path" that I have been discussing as "database consumption." Just as the snobbish otaku and the "new Homo sapiens" were two sides of the same coin in the 1980s, so were, probably, the animalized otaku and these girls in the 1990s.

The Sociality of the Otaku

In the postmodern age, people become animalized. As a matter of fact, in the past ten years the otaku have undergone rapid animalization. One reason for this is that their cultural consumption revolves not around the giving of meaning by a grand narrative but around the combination of elements extracted from the database. They no longer bother themselves with the troublesome relationship wherein "the desire of the other is itself desired"; they simply demand works in which their favorite *moe*-elements are presented in their favorite narratives.

There may be objections to such a statement, however. True, the otaku's attitude toward a work may be animalized, i.e., governed by a simple logic of lack and satisfaction. At the same time otaku are also known to be quite sociable. Far from avoiding contact with others, don't the otaku engage in diverse modes of communication, such as online chats and bulletin boards as well as conventions and "off-line meetings" in real life? And aren't there complex relationships at work, such as desiring the desire of the other? Even today, the otaku, regardless of their generation, compete with each other in collections, envy each other, boast, form cliques, and slander each other. This behavior is quite "human." Would it not be too one-sided to argue that the otaku are animalizing and that they are beginning to lose the level of desire?

But that is not the case. Indeed, the postmodern otaku are human beings equipped with desire and sociality. However, their desire and sociality are quite distant from those of the modern human beings.

As I have argued repeatedly, the otaku feel stronger "reality" in fiction than in reality, and their communication consists in large part of exchanges of information. In other words, their sociality is sustained not by actual necessity, as are kinship and local community, but by interest in particular kinds of information. Therefore, while they are quite capable of exercising their sociality as long as they can gain useful information for themselves, they always reserve the freedom to depart from the communication. Whether it is a conversation on a cell phone, an Internet chat, or instances of students or young adults not going to school or staying in their rooms,[69] such freedom "to drop out" has characterized 1990s society in general, not just in otaku culture.

In our era, most physiological needs can be satisfied immediately in an animalistic manner. Regardless of whether this contributes to our individual sense of prosperity, there is no question that in this regard contemporary Japanese society is overwhelmingly more convenient than in the past. And otaku sociality, as Miyadai has pointed out, is produced in accordance with such a society. Since sociality with the other is no longer necessary, this new sociality has no foundation in reality and is based solely on individual volition. Therefore, no matter how much otaku engage in human communication such as competition, envy, and slander, these are essentially mimicry, and it is always possible to "drop out" of them. Kojève might have explained this situation by claiming that the otaku have abandoned the substance of sociality but still maintain its form. Again, in the 1990s, this tendency was not limited to the otaku.

The Society without Grand Empathy

Indeed, the interest in small narratives, which I discussed in the previous section, has risen as if to supplement this hollowing out of sociality. In postmodernity (i.e., the animal age), the world may be understood in terms of the double-layer structure of small narratives and a grand nonnarrative, i.e., of simulacra and the database. Since there is no grand narrative in the deep inner layer, it is the small narratives in the surface outer layer that can give "meanings" for living. The database does not give us meaning. Therefore, the otaku of the 1990s are simply moved by the drama in the outer surface layer of the work, despite their desire to dissemble, analyze, and reassemble works, or *precisely because of this desire.*

The consumption of novel games is divided into double layers: the desire for the system at the level of database, and the need for drama at the level of simulacra. The former requires sociality of the otaku. They chat actively, exchange information in "off-line meetings," buy and sell derivative works, and discuss their impressions of new works. In contrast, for the latter no sociality whatsoever is required. Their needs for narratives are satisfied individually, in solitude and in absence of the other. A novel game can never be a multiplayer game. And their interest in "crying" and "*moe,*" which has quickly risen in the 1990s, clearly indicates that they are *not* expecting an emotionally moving experience or emotional identification through virtual socializing mediated by the database. In a sense, this is the commonly mentioned psychology of the otaku—the otaku, unable to be moved in reality, demand to be moved by fiction. However, there is a reason I cited concepts such as "postmodernity" and "database" in my discussion here. This change involves not only a simple shift in the locations of emotion but also a qualitative transformation.

It is unnecessary to cite Rousseau to point out that empathy was once considered a basic element of society. In a modern, tree-model society, the circuit tracing small narratives (small empathy) back to a grand narrative (a grand empathy) was still maintained. Today, emotional activities are being "processed" nonsocially, in solitude, and in an animalistic fashion. For in the postmodern, database-model society, there cannot be such a thing as a grand empathy. Today, many otaku works are clearly consumed as tools for such animalistic "processing." To this extent, the functions of *moe*-elements in otaku culture are not so different from those of Prozac or psychotropic drugs. I believe the same observation can be made of some trends in the entertainment industry, such as Hollywood films and techno music.

To conclude, corresponding to the double-layer structure of the database world, the postmodern subjectivity is also divided into double layers. This subjectivity is motivated by "the need for small narratives" at the level of simulacra and "the desire for a grand nonnarrative" at the level of database; while it is animalized in the former, it maintains a virtual, emptied-out humanity in the latter. This, in a nutshell, is the image of humanity emerging from the above observations; I call this new view of humanity *a database animal.*

The modern human was a narrative animal. People were able to satisfy their thirst for "the meaning of life" peculiar to humanity through a likewise peculiarly human means: sociality. In other words, they were able to connect small narratives with a grand narrative analogically.

However, the postmodern human cannot satisfy a thirst for "meaning" through sociality, but rather satisfies it in solitude by reducing it to animalistic needs. There is no longer any connection between small narratives and grand nonnarrative; the world drifts about materially, without giving meaning to lives. The reduction of meaning to animality, the meaninglessness of humanity, and the dissociated coexistence of the animality at the level of simulacra and the humanity at the level of database—in the language of contemporary criticism, these are my current answers to the second question of this book: After the forfeiture of the competition of transcendence in postmodernity, what will become of the humanity of human beings?

3. Hyperflatness and Multiple Personality

Hyperflatness and Hypervisuality

Postmodern Aesthetics

To some extent, the discussion to this point accomplishes my goals for this book: to analyze the present state of otaku culture from the viewpoint of postmodernity or, conversely, to investigate the essence of postmodernity through an analysis of otaku culture. I have employed such unfamiliar terms as "database," "simulacra," "a grand nonnarrative," "the double-layer structure," "the animal age," "*moe*-elements," and "dissociation" with the conviction that these concepts are useful for analyzing contemporary culture in general and are not limited to otaku culture. In any case, as someone who lived in Japan during 1990s by oscillating between contemporary thought and subculture, I found these terms imbued with a greater importance than mere concepts; I might even say they are "real" for me. As I wrote at the beginning of this book, I would be satisfied if my analysis and personal experience is convincing to many readers and contributes to their own understanding of the world.

In the present chapter, I wish to depart from theoretical discussions and instead offer some thoughts on how the postmodern world exists on the surface level and on the kind of aesthetics that govern the works in circulation there. If the previous chapters were theses on postmodern analysis, the present chapter previews their application.

The Characteristics of HTML

One such idea concerns the semiotic world of the Web. The origin of the Internet can be traced back to the 1960s, but the aggregate of all Web pages (Web sites) that we usually call "the Internet" today was born only in the 1990s. Strictly speaking, such a system, distinguished from "the Internet" (which refers to the network itself) is called the "World Wide Web" (www) or the Web. According to an entry in *The Nikkei BP Digital Encyclopedia,* the Web "is a decentralized information system in hypertext format." "Hypertext incorporates a 'link' structure, in which one can jump from a pointer within a document to another document or image. It was called the World Wide Web because it mutually links information scattered around the world in this fashion."[1]

For the sake of simplification, when I refer to the Internet from this point on in this book, I mean this world of the Web, unless noted otherwise. Now, I mentioned in the previous chapter that the structure of the Internet (including the Web) reflects the double-layer structure of postmodernity. Instead of the whole structure, however, I wish to focus solely on the surface outer layer here. When we consider the surface outer layer of the Internet, i.e., the Web pages displayed on the computer screen, first we must consider the characteristics of the HTML source code, because all Web pages, by definition, are supposed to be written in this code. No matter what is written or what kind of image is embedded, a Web page is always written in code.

HTML is a simple programming language. Originally it was used to specify the purpose of a particular element within the structure of the document vis-à-vis other elements (for example, whether a string of text is a title or a main body, or whether a certain paragraph is a block quote or not) and to convey this information to the browser. For example, in HTML the tag called <h1> is defined as a tag for a heading of the highest rank ("heading 1"). In reality, though, these features are used as tools for the Web design. Often <h1> tags are used carelessly simply to enlarge the size of a text string within the body of the text.

This usage, however, is not appropriate at all, for the ways HTML is displayed vary widely depending on the operating system and the browsers. HTML, in principle, specifies the *logical relationship* among the elements within the page, and their visual expression is left up to the user environment.[2] In other words, the <h1> tag merely specifies that a certain string of text will be read as "heading 1," without specifying the actual font size or the location. Therefore, the Web page written in the exact same HTML code often displays differently on Windows and Mac systems or between Internet Explorer and Netscape Navigator browsers. Such discrepancies are the source of headaches for those who are even moderately conscious of the design of their Web pages, whether they are specially trained Web designers or amateurs.

The World of Multiple "Visibles"

We should think of this limitation not as a flaw in the source code but as an indication of the fact that the world of the Web operates under a completely different logic than that of the print media. To simplify my explanation, let me introduce the dichotomy between "the visible" and "the invisible."

When we face a printed page, we look at the printed text and revert back into the meaning. In other words, we revert back from "the visible" into "the invisible." Conversely, when we write a text ourselves, the dominant approach is to think of it as pouring meaning into concrete strings of text—in other words, "turning the invisible into the visible."

It is well known that this approach, beyond an impressionistic view, has defined scholarship in many places from the nineteenth to the twentieth centuries. In contemporary thought this is called "phonocentrism." Although it has been discussed in a variety of ways, we will not go into the details of the discussion here. Suffice it to say that the world of print media has been operating under the logic of "making the invisible visible."

The world of the Web, however, is not constructed in this way. In it, the status of "the visible" remains in flux. Again, a series of commands written in HTML characterizes the essence of Web pages.

The screen a user confronts exists as nothing more than an "interpretation" by the user environment—that is, by the operating system, the browser, the monitor, and the video chip. Yet, the browser is not even necessary for viewing a Web page; in fact, the source code (HTML) can be opened with a text editor, as a text file including tags such as <h1>. That text file is also "visible" insofar as it is displayed as text. In this sense, there are multiple "visibles" for a Web page.

Therefore, in reading a Web page we cannot make the simple assumption that we "start with the visible" as before. More concretely, in order to judge the quality of a Web page, we cannot form our impression from one operating system, one browser, and one machine as a standard. It frequently happens that what is an excessively efficient and beautiful page in one environment cannot be displayed at all in another. Therefore, in this world the value of the "design" of a page depends not only on what is visible *but also on what is invisible;* i.e., it depends on whether the HTML language in which the page is written both loads without a hitch in as many environments as possible and retains as much of the same appearance as possible. There is a significant shift in values here. Print media starts with what is concretely visible, while the world of the Web begins with a comparative analysis of several visibles.

The Unstable Position of "The Invisible"

Furthermore, the position of "the invisible" is also unstable. For, as the example of HTML—which can also be opened as a text file—attests, on the Web something invisible in one environment (with a browser) can immediately become visible in another (with a text editor). When we are viewing a Web page with a browser, the structural information that defines the appearance is invisible. Yet that information can become visible as tags and scripts, once we look at the HTML code.

For example, if we wish to know how the layout of a Web page is constructed, the fastest way is to look at the HTML code, where all specifications are documented in concrete numbers, indicating where the tables and images are positioned and specifying what font size and background colors will be displayed. These numerical values have never been available from the layout of the printed page, unless, say, we measure it ourselves with a scale. In addition, special kinds of data not directly handled by HTML (such as the data executed by a plug-in) can also be thoroughly analyzed with an appropriate set of applications.

Moreover, HTML includes the information not only about the visible structure but also about the semantic structure. For example, in HTML there are numerous tags that directly specify the function of text strings, such as <h1> (as mentioned earlier), <dfn>, which signifies a definition of a word, and <abbr>, which signifies an abbreviation. In print media, these functions have to be conveyed indirectly through visual designs. For example, the function of <h1> must be carried out by printing the text string in a large type; <dfn> by a line break or a bold type; and <abbr> by documenting the original words in parentheses. However, HTML makes even such functions visible. In other words, the functions of each text string, which were invisible in print media, can, in principle, be turned visible once the HTML code is viewed with a text editor.[3]

The characteristic that something invisible in one environment can become visible in another is not unique to the Web, but it is common in the computer world. We are so accustomed to operating the computer by running applications through a Graphical User Interface (a "desktop" screen). However, the basis of computing is still a program written by a series of numbers and characters, and binaries underlying them. We operate a computer by "looking at" the desktop and behind that programs and binaries exist as the "invisibles."

We are not usually aware of this. However, computers have characteristics essentially to make the invisible visible immediately, if given the correct environment. It is easy to see the program behind the interface of an application, by acquiring appropriate software and decrypting the applications. (This is known as "decompiling," an operation often forbidden in reality.) We are not aware of these things when we use computers normally, but we should not ignore these fundamental characteristics if we are to consider the new culture based on computing, including the Web.

Similarities between Database Consumption and the Logic of the Web

In the world of the Web, unlike the world of print media, there are multiple "visibles," and even the position of "the invisible" is uncertain. Therefore, the conventional logic of the creator (who turns the invisible into the visible) and the receiver (who, conversely, moves back from the visible into the invisible) no longer works. For in the world of the Web, a moderately knowledgeable receiver can not only view the visible (the screen) but also transform the invisible into the visible by opening the source code.

In terms of what I discussed in the previous chapter, this act is equivalent to the user of the "novel games" analyzing the system and extracting images and scenarios. Because of this proactive participation by the user, in the world of the Web, or more generally the world of software, the unit of "a work" must be defined not only by what is visible to the user but also by what is supposed to be invisible. More concretely, the evaluation of Web pages must account for the HTML as well as the screen displayed, and the evaluation of applications must include the efficiency of the source code as well as the beauty of the interface. The culture of Web pages—perhaps because of the "page" metaphor or perhaps because so many Web sites, such as diaries and discussion boards, are still text-based—is still understood as an extension of the print culture. But it is, in essence, a culture sustained by a logic far closer to that of computer games and software.

The structure of the Internet reflects the postmodern world image. Therefore, the logic of the Web, which is produced out of this structure, is in fact not limited to the world of the Internet and computing. As everyone knows, in the past few years the terminology of various cultural forms has suddenly slid like an avalanche, seeking outward appearances that seem Internet-y and computery. As a result, the logic of the Web is penetrating widely and deeply into many other genres technologically unrelated to it.

For example, books and magazines will continue to be published in the future, but the organization and narrative style will increasingly approach those of Web pages; and movies will continue to be screened, but the direction and editing will increasingly resemble those of games and video clips. The changes in otaku culture, which I have discussed in the previous chapter, naturally emerge within this larger trend. To begin with, the behavioral pattern in database consumption, where the body of a work is understood as a database (the invisible), while the simulacra (the visibles) are extracted from it based on the preferences of the consumer, perfectly matches the logic of the Web as described above. That is why the peculiarities of the animal age are found in a condensed form in the consumption of the novel games centering around the communication on the Web.

The World of Differing Layers in Parallel

The characteristics of the worlds of the Web, computer games, and software—moreover the postmodern world in which we live—can be captured in the word "hyperflatness."[4] This expression refers, just as it sounds, to a characteristic that is thoroughly planar and yet transcends the plane. The hyperflat world, represented by the computer screen, is flat and at the same time lines up what exists beyond it in a parallel layer.

Let us consider a concrete example. Figure 20 is a screenshot taken from the desktop of the computer I am using. Here, three expressions of the same data are presented side by side. First, the window on the left of the screen is a cover image of a collection of conversations that was recently published. This image is created with a drawing application called Adobe Illustrator, and the figures in the image are all numerically specified by coordinates and vectors. Consequently, this file can be opened as a text file consisting of numerous such commands as well. The bottom-right window displays the text file.

In reality, even this text is not the true form or original of the file, since the computer processes a string of binaries and not the characters (letters and numbers) themselves. Therefore, we can display the same file in yet another method. The small window on the top right is the data portion of the same file in the hexadecimal notation, displayed with a piece of special software called a data fork editor.

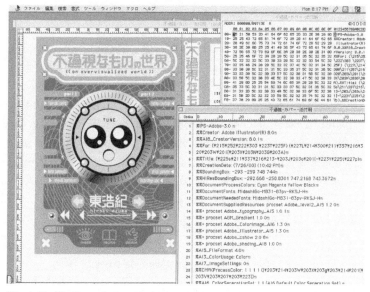

Figure 20. The "hyperflat" world of the computer desktop.

What are the relationships among these three windows? Normally, we understand this hierarchically, that the data displayed in the top-right window is the closest to the "true form," which is interpreted in a text editor as a text, which is then interpreted by Adobe Illustrator as an image. In the computer world, although such a hierarchical relationship might be correct as an explanatory principle, it has little physical ground. For if such a thing as the "true form" of a computer file exists, it is a mere electromagnetic pattern stored somewhere in hardware, and the hexadecimal notation, the text file, and the image are no different insofar as they are all an interpretation of it. It is precisely because of this that these three windows can be lined up on the same screen—or, rather, that they have to be displayed in this way.

This structure wonderfully reflects the postmodern world image. In postmodernity, the deep inner layer of the world is represented as the database, and the signs on the surface outer layer are all grasped as an interpretation (combination) of it. Therefore, in the world of simulacra, a parallel relationship (in which A, B, C, and D are all grasped as a "reading" from the same information) is preferred over a tree-like, hierarchical relationship (in which A defines B, B defines C, and C defines D, etc.).

This characteristic is not limited to the world of computing. For example, in otaku culture, as we found in our close analysis in the previous chapter, the reality is that information belonging to different layers exists side by side, such as the individual units of work like an anime or a novel, and behind those the settings and characters in their background, and in turn behind them the *moe*-elements. All such information is consumed in parallel, as equivalents, as if to open different "windows." So today's Graphical User Interface, much more than simply a useful invention, is a marvelous apparatus in which the world image of our time is encapsulated.

The Structure of Narrative Side-slipping

Furthermore, such a hyperflat world provokes a paradox, in which one cannot help pursuing the invisible *precisely because* the invisible is turned into the visible and lined up on the same plane one after another. In the example just discussed, the act of turning the invisible into the visible by changing the environment (from a drawing application to a text editor, and then to a data fork editor) is, logically speaking, a reverting back through the layers, but in its world (i.e., the desktop screen) it seems no more than a side-slipping over the same plane. Therefore, at this point another kind of desire emerges: the desire to transform as many invisibles as possible into visibles, without arriving at the agency at the final level, and to extract as many simulacra as possible from the database.

For example, because it is as easy to link to an internationally famous Web site as to link to a mere personal Web site, we wander almost necessarily from one site to another with the help of search engines. The reader who has some engagement with the world of the Internet would know that there is no intrinsic reason for the search to end. Similar modes of desire may be found in otaku culture, in the passion of trading-card collectors to "the complete" (i.e., to collect all cards in a set), in the passion of "girl games" players to check all branches, and in the passion of collectors of derivative works, which sustains numerous exhibitions and sales events of fanzines. As I touched on in the previous chapter, once the otaku are captivated by a work, they will endlessly consume related products and derivative works through database consumption. For in the database-type world they confront, there is no grand narrative that can quell that passion.

Let me try to capture the special characteristic of this desire, which works against the world of hyperflat simulacra (i.e., against the outer surface layer of postmodernity) in the term "hypervisual."[5] I use the term to mean to be "excessively visible," pointing to the quagmire in which one tries to turn the invisible into the visible endlessly and ceaselessly.[6] Earlier I discussed the dissociative cohabitation of "the desire for small narratives" and "the desire for the grand nonnarrative," but from this viewpoint we may argue that these two are connected through hypervisual relationship. This trying without success to go back from the visibles (small narratives, i.e., simulacra) to the invisible (the grand nonnarrative, i.e., database) and, instead, slipping sideways at the level of small narratives is the structure of misfire that I call "hypervisuality."

In the tree structure of modernity, the surface outer layer and the deep inner layer, or the small narratives and the grand narratives, were connected in an analogical relationship. Therefore, people were able to revert back from the former into the latter. To use the metaphors of "the visible" and "the invisible," there were first small, visible things in modernity and behind them there was a large, invisible thing; the model of the understanding of this world was to revert back from the former to the latter, by turning the invisible into visibles one after another (Figure 21a). Modern transcendence is, first and foremost, such a visual movement.

In the database world of postmodernity, however, these two are no longer directly connected. Reading the grand nonnarrative partially creates small narratives, but numerous different small narratives can be created from the same nonnarrative, and no agency exists that determines which is superior. In other words, one can revert back from small narratives to a grand nonnarrative. Therefore, what we have is an endless movement of slipping sideways, in which one tries to revert back from the small, visible things before one's eyes to the invisible, but the invisible turns into a small narrative the moment it becomes

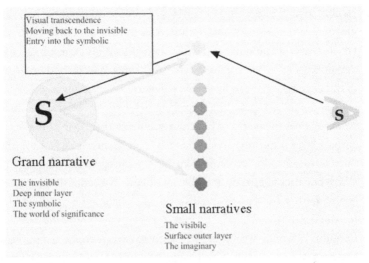

Figure 21a. Modern transcendence.

visible, and, disappointed, one heads once again for the invisible (Figure 21b). Unlike in the visual, modern transcendence, one reverts from one layer to another but will never reach a stable final level of agency in the hypervisual, postmodern transcendence. There may be many interesting philosophical questions emerging from this, but we will have to wait for another opportunity to elaborate on those developments.

Multiple Personality

Works That Make the Double-layer Structure "Visible"

In order to address the other issue, which concerns computer games, I will consider here a PC visual novel titled *Yu-No* (1996), directed by Kanno Hiroyuki (then known as Kenno Yukihiro). Kanno's works have been released mainly as "girl games," and, although they have not been widely recognized by the general public, his clever game design, spanning both the drama and the system, has won extremely high acclaim in some quarters.

At the core of Kanno's works is, in short, an emphasis on the multilayered nature of narrative. For example, in *Desire* (1994) and *Eve* (1995), he adopted an approach called "the multisight system," in

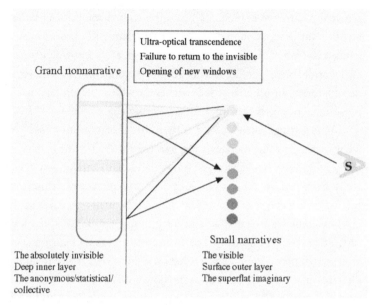

Figure 21b. Postmodern transcendence.

which one incident is viewed from the perspectives of multiple char-acters simultaneously. Also, in *The Gentleman Detective in the World of Uncertainty* (*Fukakutei sekai no tantei shinshi*, 2000), he experimented with a unique system in which several cases develop simultaneously, rather than the detective resolving one case after another. Both of these cases share not a normal multiending system in which a single narrative bifurcates into multiple branches but the idea of viewing a single narrative from multiple perspectives simultaneously. And among such attempts by Kanno, *Yu-No* is the work that is constructed in a particularly complex and careful manner.

A girl game, *Yu-No* is structurally also an adventure game with multiple storylines.[7] The basic goal of the game is to "win characters over": in this game system, there are separate scenarios for each of the five main female characters, and each scenario branches out into dif-ferent story lines, and along the way, pornographic images appear as rewards. This structure is common among many girl games, but Kanno adds an important idea. In this game, the protagonist aims not only to "win over" each woman but also to collect items spread out across the narrative branches, all in order to find the missing father. For this purpose, at the beginning of the game, the protagonist is handed an "interdimensional transporter device," to move across parallel worlds. Here "parallel worlds" refer to separate worlds with separate histories, in other words branches in which the protagonist is pursuing a love interest with different female characters.

These settings introduce a duality to the protagonist of *Yu-No*—what we might call a metalevel girl game—for the branch map of all of the story lines can be viewed even while actually dwelling in one of those branches. In the terminology I used in previous chapters, in this work the player is required to view both small narratives at the level of simulacra (the drama) and the grand nonnarrative at the level of the database (the system). The two screenshots that here are taken from actual play. Figure 22 is a screen within a parallel world, and by clicking on one of the buttons at the bottom right you get the screen shown in Figure 23, which is at the metalevel of parallel worlds. The icon within the branch map indicates where the player is within the historical timeline, and he can jump to another time or place, within certain limitations.

For the sake of the discussion in this book, it is extremely significant that a game with this structure exists. In our "animal age," the desire for small narratives at the level of simulacra and the desire for a grand nonnarrative at the level of database coexist, dissociated from each other but without contradiction. As a result, in the otaku culture of the 1990s, on the one hand otaku have pursued without reserve narratives that can efficiently move emotions and characters with which they can efficiently empathize, and on the other hand they have steadily categorized batches of *moe*-elements into databases that sustain such efficiency. In the case of *Di Gi Charat*, however, the latter realm was found only behind the work itself, in the contexts of the genre and the otaku culture as a whole. In contrast, the novel games, interestingly, contain the double-layer structure of the simulacra and the database within the works themselves and the consumers can easily access them. This is the reason why I focused on the novel games.

Yu-No takes a further, decisive step, however, in that it even makes the double-layer structure visible, displaying it on the computer

Figure 22. Screenshot of a parallel world in *Yu-No*. Produced by Elf.

screen. The player of novel games such as *The Scar* and *Air* obediently accepts individual dramas that the game system generates. The analysis of the background structure, extracting story lines and images, and the network of exchanging information and derivative works—these activities all reside outside of the game play. In other words, a clear division is established between the private satisfaction of desire for small narratives within the work and the social satisfaction of desire for the grand nonnarrative outside the work.

Yu-No, however, even incorporates into the drama itself the desire for a "completeness," which is supposed to emerge outside of the drama, and is designed to satisfy both passions within the work. In novel games, the drama is visible while the system that generates it is not; but *Yu-No* gives the illusion that both are visible.

Needless to say, even in *Yu-No,* the entire system is not visible. The branch map displayed is still just an apparent system prepared by the real system, where the important information is hidden. Therefore, consumers have also analyzed the data pack of *Yu-No,* and the otaku have had extensive communication about it. In this sense the double-layer structure of consumption applies to this work as well,

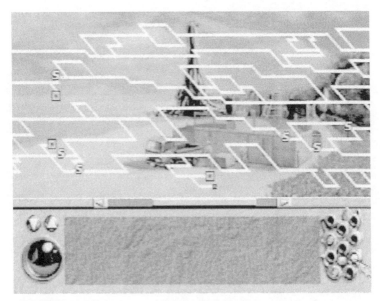

Figure 23. Screenshot of the metaparallel world in *Yu-No*.

and in this sense it is not essentially different from the aforementioned novel games. The double layering of the consumption of the drama and the consumption of the system is a precondition for computer games, and *Yu-No* cannot but fall victim to it. Still, there is no doubt that *Yu-No* is an acrobatic attempt to become conscious of that precondition despite being subsumed within it, and it is important for this reason.

The Protagonist Who Lives in a Hyperflat World

Furthermore, *Yu-No* has remarkable characteristics, not only in terms of the system but also in terms of the drama. Among them, I wish to focus on the existence of a curious premise that the protagonist's memory is *partially* lost as he moves from one parallel world to another.

This setting is not inevitable at all within the game; rather, it creates discrepancy with other settings of the game. For example, since the items collected during the travel across parallel worlds are not lost, it is unreasonable that he loses only his memory. Wouldn't the character recover his memory just by looking at the items at hand?

This contradiction is irreconcilable because in fact there is a point in the scenario when the protagonist needs an item he had already acquired in another parallel world. From the standpoint of production process, this contradiction is caused by the fact that *Yu-No* is created as a girl game and a metalevel girl game at the same time. Because it is a girl game, the protagonist must follow a world within a branch as if it is his only destiny; and because it is a metalevel girl game, the protagonist must become aware that the world is merely one of the multiple branches. This double premise brings about a contradictory situation, in which the protagonist who travels across parallel worlds loses the memory on the one hand and continues his action on the other.

Significantly, however, this situation is created not as a consequence of a failure in production but as a result of reflecting the characteristics of postmodernity all too beautifully. As I described earlier, in postmodernity it is the "hyperflat" sensibility that becomes dominant—the sensibility that lets elements from different logical levels line up as equivalent and coexist with each other. The world of *Yu-No*, in which one protagonist can be within and outside the branch at the same time, is sustained by such a sensibility. Therefore, the premise wherein the memory of a protagonist who lives in a hyperflat world periodically cuts out reflects one aspect of our age.

A Culture That Seeks Multiple Personality

That aspect is the prevalence of "multiple personality." This psychological disorder—in which multiple personalities alternately surface within one person—has become quite famous in the past decade, and there are few readers who will not have heard about it. Clinically it is called dissociative identity disorder (DID), and it has been officially recognized by the professional associations of psychiatrists. In fact, cases of this disorder were hardly ever reported before the 1950s, and even today there are few known cases outside of North America. The number of patients with multiple personality disorder rapidly increased in the United States in the 1970s; it was officially recognized in the 1980s; and in the 1990s it has even become a pervasive cultural phenomenon in Japan, featured in novels and movies. Still, its history is quite short and thin. Therefore, while there is no doubt about its existence—because there are actual patients requiring treatment—it is difficult to deny a sociological explanation in terms of the factors that produced it. In this sense, as an American philosopher of science points out, it is easier to understand multiple personality as a cultural "movement" in the late twentieth century than as a mere medical phenomenon.[8] The number of reports of multiple personality has rapidly increased and there have been many works that take multiple personality as a subject in the past three decades, not so much because of the sudden progress in psychiatry as because our society itself is strongly seeking a multiple personality–type model.

And this multiple personality–type model is precisely character-ized by a partial break of memory. The biggest reason that multiple, alternating personalities can be distinguished within a person is that there are breaks in the memory among them. Borrowing the words of Billy Milligan, who has been popularized by a book by Daniel Keyes, an alternating personality is an experience such as this: "Your're some-place doing something. Then suddenly you're someplace else, and you can tell that time has passed, but you don't know what happened."[9]

But the break can never be total. For example, it is known that if there are several alternating personalities there are often hierarchical relationships within them. In his report of the case of Milligan, Keyes depicts a scene in which two personalities, called "Arthur" and "Ragen," converse with each other, saying, "You or I. We'll share the responsi-bility. I'll spread the word to the others that no one is to allow him to take the consciousness under any circumstances."[10] This depiction itself may be too novelistic to be actually believable, but similar phenomena have been reported in articles in medical journals. For example, in a case reported in the 1970s, there were four alternating personalities, and among them A, B, and C had the complete memory of the behav-ior and psychology of D, while D was not at all aware of any of them.[11]

In short, multiple alternate personalities within a patient with multiple personality disorder are not complete "others" to each other, but they are *partial others* who share the same memory and habits in a fragmentary manner; and some of them may end up worrying about the consequences of the actions of others. With other personalities they share the same body and sometimes even part of the memory, but they insist that they have separate identities and lead separate lives.

This ambiguous sense of self may be difficult to comprehend for many readers. However, please recall the example of novel games I treated in the previous chapter. As I said earlier, the consumption of novel games consists of two layers. On the one hand, the consumer lives different destinies for each branch, and identifies with a different personality (a different aspect of the protagonist) during the game play. Personality A falls in love with woman A in destiny A; personality B with woman B in destiny B; personality C with woman C; personality D with woman D; personality E with woman E. On the other hand, the consumer has the perspective to put into relation all of these destinies, by analyzing the system and taking the screen apart into fragments.

In the previous chapter I called the coexistence of both of these "dissociation," but perhaps it is similar to the psychological structure of multiple personality as well. The player who identifies with the protagonist of a novel game at each branch partially revives the memory of having played other branches in the past but goes on to read the branch in front of him as an independent narrative. Likewise, an alternate personality within a patient diagnosed with multiple personality partially revives the memory of the lives other personalities have lived in the past but goes on to live with the sense of self at hand as its basis. There has always been an impressionistic observation that the popularity of multistory, the rise of multiending games reminds one of the pervasiveness of multiple personality, but indeed there are structural similarities between the two. Such characteristics of multiple personality–type life are concentrated in the premise of *Yu-No*'s protagonist, who oscillates among multiple branches and whose memory is often broken off while the life itself is continuous.

A Postmodern Allegory

Keeping all of these in mind, not only the premise of the protagonist but also the whole of the drama of *Yu-No* might be interpreted, curiously, as a narrative on the postmodern social structure. Let me make several points here at the end of the book, at the risk of being criti-cized as reading too much into it. For example, *Yu-No* defines the purpose of the protagonist as a pursuit of the missing father. In other words, the protagonist moves across parallel worlds while being ex-posed to split personality because of the loss of the father. These set-tings seem to allegorize postmodern characteristic features, where, after the loss of the grand narrative (the Father), small narratives coexist.

Also important here is the setting in which the protagonist can finally be reunited with his father only after successfully consummat-ing relationships with all of the female characters. Considering the case of multiple personality, this premise is an equivalent of a stan-dard therapeutic treatment for it, in which all of the alternating per-sonalities are made conscious, united, and as a result the patient re-members a trauma that caused a crisis. By jumping from one branch to another and leading the protagonist's desire to fulfillment in each world, the player of *Yu-No* is, so to speak, reunifying the protago-nist's psyche, which fell into multiple personality disorder.

Pushing this interpretation further reveals an even more interest-ing structure. In fact, the play of *Yu-No* is divided into two parts, the "Present World Episode" *(gensehen)* and the "Other World Episode" *(isekaihen)*. The stage of the drama in the former is an everyday living space, in which the protagonist is a high school student and the women are classmates, teachers, and stepmothers. This is the chapter that adopts the metalevel girl game system. In contrast, the stage of the drama in the latter episode is a typical fantasy world, where drag-ons fly across the sky and swords and magic dominate the scene. On this side, the system is that of a classic adventure game, practically without any narrative forks. These two parts are quite different in terms of the drama and the system; and, in this sense, one may argue that *Yu-No* is an aggregate of two different games.

Here it is noteworthy that these two parts get connected as the protagonist who "wins over" all female characters collects all necessary items and is ready for the reunion with the father in the "Present World Episode" is transported suddenly, without warning, to the "Other World Episode." Namely, in the world of *Yu-No*, after a successful reunification of the split mind, the Father is not resurrected but instead the fantasy world appears.

If the status of division in the "Present World Episode" were a postmodern allegory, then this sudden switch would also make clear sense. As I discussed earlier, in Japan from 1970 to 1995, many fake things were devised and consumed in order to supplement the loss of the grand narrative. The switch in *Yu-No* clearly reflects the fact that, living under the conditions of the age of fiction where people have already lost a grand narrative, an attempt to find a replacement would have to rely on a fabricated fiction. There, a realistic narrative has to develop within a small, closed space such as a "high school" or a "neighborhood." Furthermore, even if the protagonist escapes from that space and attempts to know a grand narrative that presumably resides behind the small narratives, *he can only imagine it as a world of swords and magic.* This, indeed, is the psychology that supported Aum Shinrikyō.

The protagonist who is thrown into the "Other World Episode" has already lost clues about the Father. He begins again the search for the Father, resuming a typical adventure reminiscent of role-playing games, but the protagonist encounters only women with whom he has had, or will have, sexual intercourse. In addition, the people he sees at the end of the adventure are the figure of the stepmother who sits at the seat of "Divine Emperor," where the Father is supposed to be seated, and that of her real daughter who appears there to save the stepmother. The site where the protagonist is supposed to encounter the grand narrative (the Father) is now populated with closely related women, and the protagonist will never be able to encounter the Father.

Still, the father is not quite dead, as he is supposed to be wandering in the gaps of space-time like a ghost as a "figment of imagination"; and at the end of the narrative that ghost holds a decisive option. As for the protagonist, he has sexual intercourse with the stepmother, whom his father loved, and he even has sex with the daughter, but he can save no one; and in the end he can only be transported to the edge of space-time. After going through this process, the whole of *Yu-No* comes to a full, closed circle by returning to the very first scene, without accomplishing the initial goal. Such a drama might, at first glance, seem like mere fancy; and this has its truth. Still, to me that fancy conveys the reality of our moment with an original touch—the moment in which we, after the fall of the grand narrative, have attempted and failed to reconstruct the meaning of the world, and all we can do is accrue small instances of empathy.

In any case, I believe that *Yu-No* is a work constructed with extreme care, depicting the double-layer structure of database consumption (in the system of the "Present World Episode"), the ways of life in multiple personality (in the drama of the "Present World Episode"), and the limit of fantasy in narrative consumption (in the drama of the "Other World Episode"). With words such as "postmodernity" or "otaku culture" many readers might imagine the play of simulacra cut off from social reality and self-contained in fiction, but this kind of engaged work also exists. This book was written to create a moment in which great works such as this can be freely analyzed and critiqued, without distinctions such as high culture versus subculture, academism versus otaku, for adults versus for children, and art versus entertainment. The development from this point is left to each reader.

Notes

Introduction

1. As Azuma discusses in chapter 1, the term "otaku" was already used to refer to the avid fans of anime and SF in the early 1980s, but it was with the boom of interest in the anime series *Neon Genesis Evangelion (Shin seiki evangelion)* in 1995–96, and the franchise is spawned, that otaku culture transcended the confines of cult-like fandom to become a mass social phenomenon. In addition, with the advent of such venues as the massive anonymous Japanese BBS (bulletin board system) site 2channel *(ni channeru)* and the general mainstreaming of Internet use, otaku began to communicate and engage not only with each other and to form wider communities but also with like-minded people who had hitherto not considered themselves otaku. These changes transformed the otaku community that had been suffering from the stigma promoted by the mass media in the furor surrounding the capture of a serial killer identified as an otaku by the press in the late 1980s. *Otaku* itself discusses the fringe status and later stigma that had been attached to otaku prior to 2001. However, the continued media attention itself fed not only the popularization of the term but also the eventual mainstreaming of the phenomenon and reversal of the stigma into something more celebratory signified by the runaway success of *Densha otoko* (2004–5, *Train Man*)—an otaku love story in the form of 2channel entries that was made into a best-selling novelization, a manga, a TV series, and a film starring popular celebrities of the day. Indeed the term has recently spilled into general usage in Japan to mean an over-the-top fan, hobbyist, or enthusiast of any sort; there are now, for instance, trainspotting otaku, fishing otaku, and wine otaku. All of a sudden, Japan became a nation composed wholly of otaku.

2. This figure is from a 2007 study conducted by Media Create, a media research firm. See Media kurieito [Media Create], ed., *2008 Otaku sangyō hakusho* (A whitepaper on otaku industry, 2008) (Tokyo: Media Create, 2007).

3. Alexandre Kojève, *Introduction to the Reading of Hegel,* trans. Raymond Queneau (New York: Basic Books, 1969), 158.

4. Ibid., 161–62.

5. Ibid., 162.

6. One need not mention that consumption in the United States is as often as not driven by a desire to keep up with the Joneses next door so as to acquire the status symbols of another class, the drive to own flat-screen televisions and iPhones being only the latest and certainly not last in a long line of such symbols. One need not mention that the Tokugawa peace (enabling the refinement of precisely the highly cultured realms of "Noh Theater, the ceremony of tea, and the art of bouquets of flowers" to which Kojève refers) was exactly the utopic dream of a posthistorical world by a ruling class only made possible through the "invisible" oppression of working classes, a dream that itself sets the entire snobbish culture it produced squarely into the realm of the historical. In this deeply skewed, exoticized, critical, yet widely appropriatable approach to Japan, Kojève's reading shares much with readings of Japan by his contemporaries Roland Barthes and Jacques Lacan. See Lacan's preface to the Japanese edition; "Nihon no dokusha ni yosete" (To the Japanese reader) in Jacques Lacan, *Ecrits,* vol. 1., trans. by Miyamoto Tadao, Takeuchi Michiya, Takahashi Tōru, Sasaki Takatsugu (Tokyo: Kōbundō, 1972). See also Roland Barthes, *Empire of Signs,* trans. Richard Howard (New York: Hill and Wang, 1982).

7. Furthermore, in Japan the interest in this observation by Kojève was revived in the early 1990s when Francis Fukuyama's *The End of History and the Last Man* (New York: Free Press, 1992), which mentions Kojève's view, dominated the discussion on the post–Cold War new world order. The Japanese translation of *The End of History and the Last Man* was published in the same year, but Fukuyama's views were widely discussed soon after the original article appeared in *The National Interest* in 1989, as interviews were published in such major journals as *Chūō kōron* by 1990. One can find numerous discussions on Fukuyama, Kojève, and the notion of "the end of history" by critics and intellectuals from this period. For further reflection on the notion of Japan as posthistorical see David Williams, *Japan: Beyond the End of History* (New York: Routledge, 1994).

8. In the latter half of the 1980s, Japan experienced a bubble economy, a speculative phenomenon whereby the asset prices of land and stocks were inflated well beyond their hypothetical rational market values. Generally considered to have begun in 1986, the Japanese bubble is said to have burst when in 1990 prices drastically began to fall and adjust to what many considered their more natural values.

If the previous Japan of the economic bubble period had been characterized by high consumerism predicated on the simultaneously held and contradictory assumptions of continued Japanese economic success and Western cultural dominance, the postbubble period is characterized by a sense of disillusionment with those false hopes for an ever-expanding economy and the lifelong employment that that economy was supposed to provide for its citizenry. Major events such as the Kobe earthquake and the sarin gas attacks on the Tokyo subway in 1995 solidified the sense of the deep cultural changes brought about by the economic downturn. For more on Japanese society in the post-bubble era see Tomiko Yoda and H. D. Harootunian, eds., *Japan after Japan: Social and Cultural Life from the Recessionary 1990s to the Present* (Durham, N.C.: Duke University Press, 2006), and Michael Zielenziger, *Shutting Out the Sun: How Japan Created Its Own Lost Generation* (New York: Doubleday, 2006.)

9. In *Otaku*, Azuma mentions two pioneer works on otaku culture that discuss otaku in the context of Japanese cultural tradition: Okada Toshio, *Otakugaku nyūmon* (Introduction to otaku studies) (Tokyo: Ōta Shuppan, 1996), and Ōtsuka Eiji, *Monogatari shōhiron* (Theory of narrative consumption) (Tokyo: Shin'yōsha, 1989).

10. William Kelly, ed., *Fanning the Flames: Fans and Consumer Culture in Contemporary Japan* (Albany: State University of New York Press, 2004).

11. Here *Otaku* is published by a university press. But the original Japanese edition was issued by a mainstream trade publisher.

12. Rather than over-edit and thereby excessively skew Azuma's argument and wrench it out of its messy moment of composition caught between two discursive registers, we have tried to stay close to the phrasing and pace of the text even when the argument becomes repetitive and attenuated. However, we have felt free to break up long sentences and insert subjects and do all that we deemed necessary for making the text as sensible in the English version as in the Japanese.

13. "Shingo ryūkōgo taishō" (the grand prize for neologism and buzzword of the year) is given by Jiyū Kokuminsha, the publisher of *Gendai yōgo no kisochishiki* (The basic knowledge on the contemporary terminology), the encyclopedia for current issues. The "schizo" and the "parano" won the third place for neologism in the first-ever contest in 1984. See the "Shingo ryūkōgo taishō" official Web site: http://www.jiyu.co.jp/singo/.

14. Marilyn Ivy, "Critical Texts, Mass Artifacts: The Consumption of Knowledge in Postmodern Japan," in *Postmodernism and Japan*, ed. H. D. Harootunian and Masao Miyoshi, 21–46 (Durham, N.C.: Duke University Press, 1989).

15. The journal defined the shape of critical discourse in Japan throughout much of the 1990s and remained a platform for translations of Western critical works (including Slavoj Žižek's *Tarrying with the Negative* and Derrida's *Glas*), as well as articles by Japanese critics heavily influenced by them, and reviews and roundtables on high culture.

16. Asada Akira, "Afterword," *Hihyō kūkan* (Critical space) 2nd ser., 18 (July 1998): 250.

17. Ibid.

18. In fact, although Azuma's work was certainly the most famous and the most successful work to discuss otaku culture in the language of critical theory, it was not the first attempt to do so. Ōsawa Masachi's "Otaku ron" (On otaku), a chapter in the book *Denshi media ron* (Theory of electronic media) (Tokyo: Shin'yōsha, 1995), is an earlier attempt to discuss the otaku mode of consumption compared with earlier consumer behavior in terms of the disappearance of the transcendental Other in their identities. Azuma does cite this earlier work in *Otaku.*

19. One example of this, mentioned in the text, is Okada Toshio's *Otaku-gaku nyūmon* (An introduction to otaku studies) (Tokyo: Ōta Shuppan, 1996). As Azuma observes in the main text, Okada offers an optimistic reading of otaku culture, arguing that its practitioners are advanced human beings equipped with superior vision.

20. Ōtsuka, a manga editor-turned-critic who writes widely on subculture and contemporary Japanese society, points out in his *Monogatari shōhiron* that a new mode of consumption started in the 1980s: "narrative consumption" is the consumption of products not by products themselves but by their values as signs and "narratives" that point to a larger worldview behind it. Miyadai, a sociologist who is best known for his fieldwork on high school girls called *kogal*, argues in *Owarinaki nichijō o ikiro* (Live the endless everyday) (Tokyo: Chikuma Bunko, 1998) that *kogal* are living "endless everyday" without the desire for a comprehensive understanding of the world. Ōsawa, in *Kyokō no jidai no hate* (The end of the Fictional age) (Tokyo: Chikuma Shinsho, 1996) and *Sengo no shisō kūkan* (Postwar intellectual space) (Tokyo: Chikuma Shinsho, 1998), contrasts the "idealistic age" of the 1960s and the "fictional age" after the 1970s to describe the shift in political and social imagination—and names the believers of Aum Shinrikyō as a typical example of those living in "the age of fiction." Ōsawa also discusses the sociology of electronic communication in *Denshi media ron.*

21. It is, perhaps, too easy for translators to claim that a book was already a translation before they began their work, and yet this seems especially true of Azuma's original, which already translated otaku consumer behavior into postmodern theory.

22. Asada Akira, "J-kaiki no yukue" (Whither 'J-turn'?), *Voice*, March 2000. "J" represents "Japan," as in "J-pop" or "J-league," and this essay, published before the publication of *Otaku*, discusses Azuma's turn to the subject of otaku in the context of other younger critics' turn to Japan-related topics around 2000. In the same year after the publication of Asada's article, Azuma

states, he received a "violent personal attack" from Asada, apparently referring to the article, and in turn Azuma launched a damning criticism of *Hihyō kūkan* as a whole. See Azuma, "Gojōkyōron," *Shōsetsu torippā*, June 2000; repr. in Azuma, *Bungaku kankyō ronshū Azuma Hiroki korekushon L* (Essays on literary environment: Azuma Hiroki collection L) (Tokyo: Kōdansha, 2007), 508–21. Azuma continued his attacks against Karatani and Asada on occasion: see, for example, Azuma's remark on Karatani's post-9/11 response in a dialogue with critic Kasai Kiyoshi in *Dōbutsuka suru sekai no nakade* (In the animalizing world) (Tokyo: Shūeisha Shinsho, 2003). Asada and Karatani largely neglected responding to these attacks. Reflecting on this episode, Azuma writes that he was "purged" from *Hihyō kūkan* (see *Bungaku kankyō ronshū*, 498), but, to be fair, the harsh, often mocking and belittling tone of Azuma's criticism in these essays might lead us to assume that Azuma is in part responsible for the parting of ways. The spat even grabbed public interest. The sensationalist response of the Japanese media itself can be seen as symptomatic of the personality-driven intellectual culture of contemporary Japan.

23. Positive early reviews in literary journals and newspapers that squarely tackle Azuma's polemics include those by Suga Hidemi (*Voice*, February 2002: 214–15), Ōsawa Masachi (*Yomiuri shinbun*, January 27, 2002: 12), and Takahara Eri (*Bungakukai*, February 2002: 298–300). These reviews also already point to areas that Azuma left for future discussions: the activities of female otaku (this glaring lack is mentioned in one of Azuma's own footnotes) and the otaku as a class issue (the issues that became more relevant in recent years as many Japanese young people struggle financially as "working poor").

24. As he states on his Web site, Azuma's present interests may be "divided into two directions": "toward the transformation of literary imagination under postmodernization / otaku-ization" and toward "the idea of liberty / freedom of humans living under the emergence of ubiquitous information society." This dialectic invigorates his writing with a vibrant symbiosis evident most clearly in his collaborative work with various activists and entrepreneurs outside academia that transcends the confines of academia toward mass culture. In this regard see his series of articles entitled "Jōhō jiyūron" (On freedom of information) on the relations of information technologies and freedom of information in *Chūō kōron* (Central review), which will be included in his forthcoming collection *Jōhō kankyōronshū* (Essays on information environment) (Tokyo: Kōdansha, 2007). See also Azuma and Ōsawa Masachi, *Jiyū o kangaeru: 9.11 go no gendai shisō* (Thinking liberty: Post-9/11 contemporary thoughts) (Tokyo: NHK Books, 2003), a collaborative that searches for a new freedom in a world of complicity and animalistic fears and combines many of Azuma's observations on pop culture with his deeper concerns for the future of liberty. Also, Azuma was long involved in ISED, a forum for the discussion on "Interdisciplinary

Studies on Ethics and Design of Information Society," featuring academics, IT entrepreneurs and engineers, IT lawyers, and bloggers. The proceedings of ISED can be found at http://www.glocom.jp/ised/.

25. Karatani Kojin, "Aironī naki owari" (The end without irony), in *Kindai bungaku no owari* (The end of modern literature) (Tokyo: Inscript, 2005), 193, 195.

26. Hiroki Azuma, *Gēmu teki riarizumu no tanjō: Dōbutsuka suru posuto-modan 2* (A birth of gamelike realism: Animalizing postmodernity 2) (Tokyo: Kōdansha Gendai Shinsho, 2007).

27. Hiroki Azuma, "A preface for Karatani Kōjin," in *Hyūmoa to shiteno yuibutsuron* (Materialism as humor) (Tokyo: Kōdansha Gakugei Bunko, 1999); reprinted as Hiroki Azuma, "Karatani Kōjin ni tsuite II" (On Karatani Kōjin II), in *Yūbinteki fuan tachi #*, 345–53 (Postal anxieties #) (Tokyo: Asahi Bunko, 2002), 353.

28. It should be noted that, although the Japanese word *dōbutsu* (animal), like its Western counterparts, contains etymologic meaning referring to movement, it shares none of the phonetic similarity animal and anime. *Anime* is, of course, a Japanization of the English word *animation*, but few Japanese readers would be conscious of its historic relation to the notion of motion as in *motion* pictures. In Japanese, an old term for motion pictures, *katsudō shashin*, does contain a linguistic similarity to *dōbutsu* (they both share the character *dō* meaning "movement"). But the general contemporary term for films or movies in Japanese is *eiga*, which does not contain the nuance of movement but rather refers prominently to projection. So our translation of *dōbutsu* as animal and *anime* as anime may falsely accentuate a link not necessarily implied in the original.

29. Akira Mizuta Lippit, *Electric Animal: Toward a Rhetoric of Wildlife* (Minneapolis: University of Minnesota Press, 2000), 165. See also Lippit, "Magnetic Animal: Derrida, Wildlife, Animetaphor," *MLN* 113, no. 5, Comparative Literature Issue (December 1998): 1111–25; and "Afterthoughts on the Animal World" *MLN* 109, no. 5, Comparative Literature (December 1994): 786–830.

1. The Otaku's Pseudo-Japan

The translation of chapter 1 is based on a translation by Julia Yonetani and Minoru Hokari. We gratefully acknowledge their work and contribution.—Trans.

1. ["J-pop" refers to Japanese popular music, especially that after the 1990s.—Trans.]

2. [Derived from the English "costume play," *kosupure* (or its re-Anglicization, "cosplay") refers to the act of dressing up in the costume of an

anime or game character. While the current usage in English almost exclusively refers to nonsexual activities at anime- or game-fan events, the connotation in Japanese still carries a tinge of sexual innuendo, as it also continues to be used to describe the sexual role-play practiced in sex parlors.—Trans.]

3. ["Novel games"—also known as "visual novels" in Japanese—are a computerized form of interactive fiction (IF). Although comparisons to gamebooks may be apt in their placing choices of narrative branches in the hands of readers/players, this particular Japanese subgenre of IF is, according to Azuma, distinct in its architectonics of desire. Several "novel games" are discussed in chapter 3.—Trans.]

4. [In 1988 and 1989, four girls between the ages of four and seven were kidnapped and murdered in Tokyo and Saitama, and Miyazaki was arrested in July 1989 as a suspect in these crimes. A media circus ensued, in which the suspect's troubled psychiatric state and his intense interest in otaku culture such as anime and horror films were closely reported; TV news and talk shows repeatedly played the image of Miyazaki's room overflowing with anime videotapes and comics. As Azuma explains, throughout the 1990s Miyazaki became a public face of sorts for the otaku, casting a negative image of otaku not only as immature social misfits but also as perverts and threats to society.—Trans.]

5. The expression "otaku" as we currently use it (to refer to a subculture group) was first employed by Nakamori Akio in 1983. See Nakamori Akio, *Otaku no hon* (A book of otaku) (Tokyo: JICC, 1989). It is said that the use of "otaku" as a nickname, from which this current use derives, dates back to science fiction fandom in the 1960s.

6. *Shūkan Yomiuri* (Yomiuri weekly), September 10, 1989, as discussed in Nakamori, *Otaku no hon,* 90.

7. [Okada Toshio (b. 1958), the former CEO of Gainax—an anime and video game production company—and an avid collector himself, has written and lectured extensively on otaku culture and is widely regarded as a spokesperson for the otaku.—Trans.]

8. Okada Toshio, *Otakugaku nyūmon* (An introduction to otaku studies) (Tokyo: Ōta Shuppan, 1996), 10, 49. [The term "new type" is apparently borrowed from the notion of an evolved form of human being in the anime series *Mobile Suit Gundam.*—Trans.]

9. [Azuma is probably referring to the series of negative comments by Asada Akira, an editor of the critical journal *Hihyō kūkan* (Critical space), around 1999 and 2000. For Azuma's reaction to Asada's comments, see "Gojōkyōron," no. 2 (On erroneous circumstances, no. 2) *Shōsetsu torippā* (Summer 2006); reprinted in *Bungaku kankyō ronshū: Azuma Hiroki korekushon L* (Essays on literary environment: Azuma Hiroki collection L) (Tokyo: Kōdansha,

2007), 508–21. See the Translators' Introduction in this book for more discussion of the critical scene in the 1980s and the '90s as the background of this rift.—Trans.]

10. [Azuma debuted in the Japanese critical scene with "Solzhenitsyn shiron" (A note on Solzhenitsyn) in *Hihyō kūkan* 1st ser., 9 (March 1993). *Hihyō kūkan* was the premier journal on critical theory in Japan through much of the 1990s, and Azuma contributed to the journal for several years. See Translators' Introduction for more on Azuma's relationship with *Hihyō kūkan*.—Trans.]

11. [The suffix "-*kei*" 系 is rendered in this translation as "-related," to suggest the sense of "system," "relationship," and even "kinship," all of which are connoted in the kanji character. In the current usage, though, the suffix is casually used among the otaku and the younger generation of Japanese to point to a general association with a place or an idea, as in *Akihabara-kei* or *Akiba-kei* (the fashion trends or tastes of those gathered in Akihabara; Azuma uses this term in note 13 of this chapter) or *Sekai-kei* (the kind of plot in anime and video games in which the small group of characters act as if their thoughts and actions can affect the fate of the entire world, which, incidentally, Azuma has discussed extensively in recent years). Though Azuma uses "otaku-kei bunka" or literally "otaku-related culture" throughout, after this first explanation in the text, we have chosen to translate this term as simply "otaku culture" because the term "otaku" in English already seems to connote the wider range of products and modes of production Azuma is including in his term.—Trans.]

12. According to Takekuma Kentarō, one origin of otaku culture lies in the activities in the 1960s of Ōtomo Shōji. Ōtomo, who in 1973 died suddenly at the age of thirty-seven, was a columnist and editor, as well as being known as instigator of the boom in monster movies and TV shows. He made his debut in mass media in 1961 and from 1966 to 1971 wrote many articles for the *Shōnen Magajin* about monsters, mysteries, science fiction, occult, robots, and computers, topics that would later form the core of otaku culture.

13. One such example is the kind of rapid otaku-fixation with Akihabara pointed out by Morikara Kaichirō. In the 1990s, Akihabara was known neither for electronic goods nor computers but developed into a unique area that worked to create a fusion of the information industry and subculture. Although I will not go into them at length here, in the aforementioned *Di Gi Charat* and the Ōtsuki Toshimichi–produced *Cyber Team in Akihabara (Akihabara dennōgumi)*, otaku works in the 1990s are strongly connected to the town of Akihabara. This contrasts with the 1970s and 1980s, when otaku culture was connected to the cityscape along the Chuo train line. In this sense—in the same sense as a particular type of person is associated with Shibuya, Shinjuku, and Shimokitazawa—otaku culture in the 1990s may also perhaps

be referred to as '*Akihabara-kei*' ("Akihabara-related"). [See note 11 for this usage of -kei—Trans.]

14. Even more specifically, this book focuses on the activities of male otaku of the third generation. As symbolized by the fact that the Comic Market has long been split over two days, at some unknown point becoming separated into male comics and female comics, the gender divide in otaku culture cannot be ignored. This issue, however, is not touched on in this work.

15. [For Azuma's more in-depth discussion of postmodernity, see, for example, "Posuto modan saikō: sumiwakeru hihyō II" (Rethinking the postmodern: Cohabitation of criticism II), in *Yūbin teki fuantachi #*, 29–50 (Postal anxieties #) (Tokyo: Asahi Bunko, 2002).—Trans.]

16. [Ōtsuka Eiji (b. 1958), scriptwriter and former editor of many comic books, has established himself as a major figure in the world of subculture, writing from the perspective of a creator. As a cultural critic, he has written on subjects ranging from literature to anthropology to politics.—Trans.]

17. [*Sekai* ("a world") is the term used to describe codified texts, settings, images, or patterns of action employed within kabuki and *bunraku* puppet theater. *Shukō* ("a plan, idea, or set of devices") refers to the new twist (e.g., plot, character, setting) then added to the original *sekai*. Through this creative process of transformation, the *sekai* is thus first fragmented by and then readjusted according to new *shukō*.—Trans.]

18. Ōtsuka Eiji, *Monogatari shōhiron* (Theory of narrative consumption) (Tokyo: Shin'yōsha, 1989), 20–24; and Okada, *Otakugaku nyūmon* (An introduction to otaku studies) (Tokyo: Ōta Shuppan, 1996), 224ff. [Edo, the old name for the city of Tokyo, also used to refer to the period of relative peaceful rule of the Tokugawa Shōgunate for more than two hundred and sixty years between 1603–1867. "Urbanity" or *iki* refers to the sense of urban connoisseurship developed during the Edo period, especially among the upscale merchants who would frequent pleasure quarters. Inspired by his study under Martin Heidegger, the philosopher Kuki Shūzō (1888–1941) famously explicated the term as a quintessence of Japanese taste in '*Iki*' *no kōzō* (The structure of 'Iki') (1930). According to Kuki, *iki* exhibits three main traits: *bitai* or allure, *hari* or haughtiness, and *akirame* or resignation. See Hiroshi Nara, *The Structure of Detachment: The Aesthetic Vision of Kuki Shūzō* (Honolulu: University of Hawai'i Press, 2004).—Trans.]

19. See Murakami's essay "Sūpāfuratto nihon bijutsu ron" (A theory of superflat Japanese art) in Murakami Takashi, ed., *Sūpāfuratto* (Tokyo: Madora Shuppan, 2000). Murakami Takashi touched on the analogy between figurines and Buddhist sculptures in a speech during Wonder Festival 2000, on August 20, 2000. [Kanō Sansetsu (1589–1651) is a painter of the early Edo period who belonged to the Kanō school. Soga Shōhaku (1730–81) is a painter of the mid–Edo period.—Trans.]

20. [Ayanami Rei is a popular female character from *Neon Genesis Evangelion.*—Trans.]

21. If we look at magazine culture, manga, or anime, each in turn, U.S. influence dates back to at least the 1930s. This accumulation of influence in fact had a large impact on the development of otaku culture in the postwar era. For example, in recent years it has become more and more apparent that various techniques previously thought to have been developed by Tezuka Osamu were in fact inherited from prewar cartoonists. However, it is certain that this influence was suspended with the onset of World War II and redeveloped in the postwar period under completely different conditions. Otaku culture emerged as a coherent subculture after this time.

22. Stated by Mori Takuya. See Mori, *Animeeshon nyūmon* (Introduction to animation) (Tokyo: Bijutsu Shuppansha, 1966), 30–31.

23. Suggested by Oguro Yūichirō in a conversation.

24. [Komike or Comiket is the largest amateur comic book convention in Japan, held every six months.—Trans.]

25. [For the figures of *miko* in anime and manga, see Patrick Drazen, *Anime Explosion!* (New York: Stone Bridge Press, 2002), 164–68.—Trans.]

26. Sawaraki Noi, *Nihon, gendai, bijutsu* (Japanese, modern, art) (Tokyo: Shinchōsha, 1998), 94ff. [Sawaraki argues that what enabled "schizophrenic Japanese pop" in the 1990s was not the proliferation of worldwide subculture but the "Japanese" question—namely the cultural "occupation" of American pop in postwar Japan—that casts a long, ominous shadow over the seemingly apolitical Japanese pop art in the 1990s.—Trans.]

27. [Asada Akira's *Kōzō to chikara* (Structure and power) (Tokyo: Keisō Shobō, 1983) is a lucid introduction to postmodernist thought, especially that of Jacques Lacan and Gilles Deleuze. Despite the subject matter, it became an instant bestseller in 1983 and was considered at the heart of the "new academism." See Translators' Introduction to this book for further discussion on the impact Asada has had on the discussion on postmodernism in the 1980s Japan.—Trans.]

28. [See Translators' Introduction for an extensive discussion on "New Academism."—Trans.]

29. See Azuma, "Posuto modan saikō." This essay is available on my personal Web site, http://www.hirokiazuma.com/. [The piece is no longer available on his Web site, but the revised version, "Posuto modan saikō: sumiwakeru hihyō II" (Rethinking the postmodern: Cohabitation of criticism II), is included in *Yūbin teki fuantachi #* (Postal anxieties #) (Tokyo: Asahi Bunko, 2002).—Trans.]

30. See, for example, Karatani Kōjin "Hihyō to posutomodan" (Criticism and the postmodern), in *Sai to shite no basho* (Location as difference) (Tokyo: Kōdansha Gakujutsu Bunko, 1996), 125–73.

31. ["Kindai no chōkoku" (Overcoming modernity) is the title of a round-table discussion published in the September and October 1942 issues of *Bunga-kukai* (Literary world). The critic Kawakami Tetsutarō organized the round-table featuring thirteen intellectuals including the literary critics Kobayashi Hideo and Kamei Katsuichirō as well as philosophers, scholars of religion, and writers. Participants discussed a wide range of issues related to "over-coming modernity," but the participants who attracted the most scholarly at-tention were the "Kyoto School" philosophers such as Nishitani Keiji, who argued for the limitations of Western civilization based on individualism and Japan's "mission" to lead the rest of Asia and the world based on the new phi-losophy that combines the philosophies of the East and the West. As a whole, it is difficult to find a common conclusion among all participants, but later critics saw this roundtable as a justification of the Japanese war effort fought under the banner of ultranationalism and anti-Westernism. Postwar thinkers and philosophers such as Takeuchi Yoshimi, Hiromatsu Wataru, and Karatani Kōjin all had extensive discussion on the legacy of this roundtable. Karatani writes in the afterword for Hiromatsu's *"Kindai no chōkoku" ron* (On "over-coming modernity"): "The topic of 'overcoming modernity' is doubly signifi-cant for us—first all, because we are still living in 'modernity' that should be overcome; and secondly because we have not yet gone beyond the prewar problematic of 'overcoming modernity' in an essential way." Hiromatsu Wataru, *"Kindai no chōkoku" ron* (Tokyo: Kōdansha Gakujutsu Bunko, 1989), 272. See also Harry Harootunian, *Overcome by Modernity: History, Culture, and Community in Interwar Japan* (Princeton, N.J.: Princeton University Press, 2000).—Trans.]

32. [Alexandre Kojève (1902–1968) was a Russian-born Hegelian philo-sopher whose legendary lectures on Hegel's *Phenomenology of Spirit* (pub-lished as Alexandre Kojève and Raymond Queneau, *Introduction to the Reading of Hegel* [New York: Basic Books, 1969]) influenced many twentieth-century French philosophers from Jean-Paul Sartre and Jacques Lacan to Michel Foucault and Jacques Derrida. Azuma discusses a footnote to Kojève's lecture on *Phenomenology of Spirit* in which Kojève proposes the notions of Japanese snobbery and American animalization. See Translators' Introduction to this volume for more extensive discussion on the impact of this footnote in Japan around 1990.—Trans.]

33. In fact, this work includes a highly suggestive plot for comprehend-ing the extent to which a sense of political direction was lacking in 1980s Japan. The Tokyo of *Megazone 23* is, as noted here, a mere fiction created by a spaceship's computer. This becomes clear as the "military" assumes control of the computer in order to resist the enemy, who appears from outside the spaceship. However, the "military" do not divulge to the people of Tokyo that the enemy has come from outer space and to the end continue to pretend

they are at war with "a country." As the political message of the work (a criticism against increasing right-wing tendencies) becomes clear, this far-out setting reveals people's thinking at the time. It is certain that Japan began moving to the right from the mid-1980s and that this trend continued into the 1990s. But what they are reacting against, exactly who was the oncoming enemy, and exactly who would thus benefit? Thus the creators of *Megazone 23* could only position the real sense of crisis they felt against an unrealistic backdrop. Precisely this—an enemy appearing from beyond a spaceship—was the bizarre atmosphere that existed in the 1980s.

34. ["Enjo kōsai" (compensated dating) is the term the media used in the 1990s to describe Japanese schoolgirls dating and sometimes having sex with much older men for money. The term is often used as a euphemism for underage prostitution but could also be used when sex is not involved. This phenomenon was reportedly widespread among teenagers in the cities and linked with the rise in the use of cell phones. The Japanese media remained fascinated with this phenomenon, but the extent of the problem is unknown, in part because of its underground nature. Whether the media's role in creating the hype is justified has been the subject of debate. See David Leheny, *Think Global, Fear Local: Sex, Violence, and Anxiety in Contemporary Japan* (Ithaca, N.Y.: Cornell University Press, 2006) for the discussion on how the "enjo kōsai" phenomenon was linked to Japanese Diet's adoption of international ban of child prostitution and child pornography. "Gakkyū hōkai" (literally "the classroom breakdown") was a phenomenon in Japanese elementary schools in the 1990s, in which the classroom ceased to function as a group for an extended period of time, because students did not obey their teachers' instructions. In such classrooms, it was reported, students could not sit still, continued talking among themselves while their teachers were speaking, and even verbally insulted and abused their teachers. In a study published in 2003, 32 percent of the public elementary schoolteachers surveyed answered that they experienced such a situation in their classroom. The reasons for this phenomenon are manifold and complex—critics have cited the teachers' lack of classroom management skills, the lack of institutional strategy to tackle the issue, learning disabilities such as attention deficit hyperactivity disorder, and the parents' general uncooperativeness—and the phenomenon received a overabundance of media attention.—Trans.]

35. Okada, *Otakugaku nyūmon*, 230ff; Murakami, Foreword, in *Sūpāfuratto*; Sakamoto Ryūichi and Murakami Ryū, *E. V. Café* (Tokyo: Kōdansha Bunko, 1989), 351.

36. [The term *moe* is used within otaku jargon to refer to the strong sense of sympathy felt toward anime characters. Within the otaku world, *moe* has come to point to a longing for something in particular. As the literal meaning of *moe* is "bud," the term still bears some of the weight of its early

usage when it primarily referred to the interest in the sprout-like hair emerging from some characters' heads. It literally means "sprouting," but it is a recent neologism among the otaku to connote the strong emotion triggered by an image or a character. Etymological origins of the word are obscure, but it is said to stem from an incorrect kanji conversion for another word pronounced "*moe*," which means "burning" (as in the burning of a heart or passion). The usage apparently gained popularity among the online otaku communities that take pleasure in using such a wordplay involving a playful and sometimes intentionally incorrect kanji conversion. While "burning" *moe* means all-out, burning passion, "sprouting" *moe* might suggest a more gentle, benign feeling for a cute object, although the desire can be (and often is) sexual. Yet "lust," too, is an inadequate translation for *moe*, which can be said to reside both in the character being described (as in that character has a number of *moe* traits) and within the consumer (as in he has *moe* for that character). Some translators have opted for "affect," but as the untranslated word itself rapidly gains currency among the English-language otaku (like the word *otaku*) we have chosen to use the word transliterated to best convey its full range of meanings. The term is grammatically flexible: one can simply "*moe*-ru" (in the verb form), or feel "*moe*" for something, while "*moe*-elements" (Azuma's neologism) are attributes of the object. See chapter 2, section 5 for Azuma's discussion of *chara-moe* or *moe* toward characters. —Trans.]

37. ["Girl games," or *gyaru gē*, is a type of adventure game often including the simulation of romantic relations and erotic scenes involving a young female character. Azuma discusses these games more extensively in chapter 2, section 8. —Trans.]

38. [The Genroku period (1688–1704) is considered the height of economic prosperity during the Edo period. It is also known for a flourishing in literature and arts, dominated by the lavish and decadent tastes of rich merchants. The term "Shōwa Genroku" refers to the cultural and economic boom during the 1960s and '70s in Japan, comparable to the Genroku period. —Trans.]

39. [*Imekura* or "image clubs" are a sex parlors in which the women providing sexual services dress in various costumes—such as high schoolers' or nurses' uniforms—to cater to the specific fantasies of the male customers.—Trans.]

40. [Kobayashi Yoshinori (b. 1953) is best known today for his conservative, anti-American political-commentary-in-manga series *Gōmanizumu sengen* (Haughtiness-ism manifesto, 1992–). In particular, published as a special issue of the series, *Sensōron* (On war) (Tokyo: Gentōsha, 1998, 2001, 2003) provoked controversy for his unabashed defense of Japanese prewar militarism. Before his *Gōmanizumu* fame, he was known as (and he still considers himself) a popular and prolific author of comedy manga, such as *Tōdai icchokusen* (Straight into University of Tokyo, 1976) and *Obocchama kun* (Little princeling,

1986). Fukuda Kazuya (b. 1960) is a literary critic and political commentator. Initially a specialist in French literature, he contributes to a wide range of media from the classy literary journal *Bungei shunjū* to the hip and trashy magazine *SPA!*, mixing generally conservative politics and an often provocative style— and giving himself a nickname "the fascist right-wing punk." Torihada Minoru is a comedian known for his deadpan imitation of a low-rank, right-wing activist giving street speeches in a military uniform. His performance in theaters has had a cult following despite the fact that he rarely appears on television.—Trans.]

2. Database Animals

1. For more on the Baudrillardian notion of "simulacra," see, for example, Jean Baudrillard, *Symbolic Exchange and Death* (London: Sage Publications, 1993), and Jean Baudrillard, *Simulacra and Simulation, The Body, in Theory* (Ann Arbor: University of Michigan Press, 1994).

2. [The Japanese term *sofuto* encompasses a wider range than the English word *software*. So Azuma's usage refers both to computer programs specifically and to intellectual and cultural products or content more generally.—Trans.]

3. [The Japanese term *moratoriamu* derives from the English "moratorium." In Japanese, it is generally used to refer to the stage of young adulthood in Erik Erikson's theory of psychosocial development—specifically, the period of limbo between high school and the first employment.—Trans.]

4. [Italics here refer to the hiragana phoneticization, rather than the otaku as the katakana word or the kanji word, and is used as one of numerous second-person pronouns in modern Japanese, and literally means "your home" or "your family." Before otaku began to use this personal pronoun frequently, it was used in a rather formal context, by virtue of its indirect reference to the household.—Trans.]

5. Nakajima Azusa, *Kommyunikēshon fuzen shōkōgun* (Communication deficiency syndrome) (Tokyo: Chikuma Bunko, 1995), 44, 49.

6. The most fundamental work on the "decline of the grand narrative" is Jean-François Lyotard, *Postmodern Condition* (Minneapolis: University of Minnesota Press, 1984). The analysis of this book mainly concerns changes in the academic world, but the interpretation of this term coined by Lyotard has been stretched and it has been circulating as a useful concept for grasping the characteristics of the world since the 1970s. Hence, the term "the decline of the grand narrative" in this book is used as an extended concept, including various such extended interpretations, rather than the original concept of Lyotard.

7. [The oil shocks of 1973 and 1974 resulted in global inflation and stagflation. Japan witnessed surging wholesale prices. The Japanese economy stagnated. The United Red Army was a radical group responsible for the Asama-Sansō hostage crisis in late February 1972, when five members of the group

took over a mountain lodge and kept the manager's wife hostage. The stand-off with police, lasting ten days, was a national media story culminating with live coverage of the siege. See P. G. Steinhoff, "Hijackers, Bombers, and Bank Robbers: Managerial Style in the Japanese Red Army," *Journal of Asian Studies* 48 (November 1989): 724–40.—Trans.]

8. Ōsawa Masachi, "Otaku ron" (On otaku), in *Denshi media ron*, 242–93 (Theory of electronic media) (Tokyo: Shin'yōsha, 1995), 259ff.

9. [Is Ōsawa's discussion on otaku cited here implicitly linking otaku with the Aum Shinrikyō? Although Ōsawa's "On Otaku" does not directly address the Aum Shinrikyō phenomenon and was probably written before the sarin gas attack of 1995, Ōsawa explains in the preface of *Denshi media ron* that the book was edited and published amid the media frenzy surrounding the gas attack and the cult group and strongly suggests the contemporary relevance of his discussion in the book.—Trans.]

10. ["Bikkuriman choko" ("Surprise-Man chocolate") is a cheap choco-late snack that became immensely popular in the 1980s because of a sticker enclosed in each package. The stickers portray various fictitious characters that inhabit the "Bikkuriman World"; and there are rare, premium "shiny" stickers. The stickers became collectors' items and parents raised eyebrows as children purchased the snack just for the stickers and threw away the choco-late wafer; its popularity spawned several comic and anime series.—Trans.]

11. [*Mobile Suit Gundam* and *Saint Seiya* were popular anime series from the late 1970s and the 1980s, both famous for their extensive families of character products—robots called mobile suits for *Gundam* and superheroes for *Seiya*. Onyanko Club was a popular teenage girls' group from the Japanese TV show in the mid-1980s. The group consists of a few dozen "members," and because of the sheer size of the group the members are often identified by "membership numbers." While many of the girls are not particularly skilled as singers, a fan can find for himself his favorite "girl next door" from the diverse group by following individual members and learning about them, in a similar way that one "collects" the Bikkuriman stickers.—Trans.]

12. Ōtsuka, *Monogatari shōhiron*, 13–14, 17–18, 18–19.

13. [Two words Azuma uses, *sekaizō* and *sekaikan*, are both usually ren-dered in English simply as "worldview." However, we have found it necessary to use "world image" and "worldview" to differentiate the two as they seem to stem directly from Heidegger's use of *Weltbild* and *Weltanschauung*, respec-tively. In this regard, it is significant to note that Azuma was particularly aware of Heidegger's notion that "Animals are lacking in world *(weltarm),*" having published an article on Derrida's reading of this statement the same year that the Japanese version of *Otaku* was published. See Azuma, "Sōzōkai to dōbutsuteki kairo: keishikika no Derrida teki shomondai" (The imaginary and the animalistic circuit: Derridean issues of formalization) in *Bungaku*

kankyō ronshū: Azuma Hiroki korekushon L (Essays on literary environment: Azuma Hiroki collection L) (Tokyo: Kōdansha, 2007). Also see Jacques Derrida, *Of Spirit: Heidegger and the Question,* trans. Geoffrey Bennington and Rachel Bowlby (Chicago: University of Chicago Press, 1989).

The Japanese term *settei,* translated here as "settings," has a broad range of meanings. According to the *Kenkyūsha's New Japanese–English Dictionary* (5th edition), *settei* means "establishment; creation; institution; fixation." But the word is used rather differently in the computer world. Since its inclusion into the Japanese-localized versions of the Mac operating system menus in the late eighties, the term has come to take on the added meanings of "configurations," "preferences," "settings," "properties," "characteristics," and "data." In the realm of narratology, *settei* has come to be associated with the settings of a narrative that constitutes a fictional world—including everything from the time period, the place, and character relations to physical features such as height, weight, and eye and hair color. We have therefore chosen *settings* to capture the widest possible range of meanings.—Trans.]

14. The most useful work for understanding the characteristics of the rhizome model is Asada Akira's *Structure and Power*; the chart on pages 236–37 of that volume is particularly useful. Incidentally, according to Asada, the tree model represents premodern society, while modern society is represented by the Klein bottle; but I would argue that these are two sides of the same system, and together they maintain the tree model. If you are interested in the philosophical details of this point, please see my *Ontological, Postal (Sonzaironteki, yūbinteki)* (Tokyo: Shinchōsha, 1998). In that book I called the tree model "the metaphysical system" and the Klein-bottle model "the negative theology system." [Gilles Deleuze and Félix Guattari elaborate on the "rhizome," a figure representing a heterogeneous, centerless, ever-changing network (as a model for postmodern worldview) in "Rhizome," in *A Thousand Plateaus* (Minneapolis: University of Minnesota Press, 1987), 3–25. Deleuze and Guattari are two of the key figures in Asada's survey of postmodernism in *Structure and Power*; the chart in this book that Azuma mentions here contrasts premodernity, modernity, and postmodernity, and here "rhizome" offers the principal figure for postmodernity. In *Ontological, Postal,* Azuma contrasts "the metaphysical system" and "the negative theology system" with the "postal" deconstruction of the late Derrida. See chapter 4 of *Ontological, Postal,* 213–335.—Trans.]

15. [The original Japanese here is *yomikomi moderu.* The verb *yomikomu* means "to load," as data into a database, but it also means "to read thoroughly and voraciously," "to read into," or even "to overinterpret," as a text.—Trans.]

16. [For an English-language overview of how the members of Aum Shinrikyō and the commentators of Aum view the role of manga and anime in relation to Aum, see Richard A. Gardner, "Aum Shinrikyō and a Panic about

Manga and Anime," in *Japanese Visual Culture*, ed. Mark W. MacWilliams, 200–18 (Armonk, N.Y.: M. E. Sharpe, 2008).—Trans.]

17. Ōsawa Masachi, *Kyokō no jidai no hate* (The end of the fictional age) (Tokyo: Chikuma Shinsho, 1996), 52ff.

18. Ōtsuka, *Monogatari shōhiron*, 26ff.

19. [*Zengaku kyōtō kaigi* (Congress for all-campus joint struggle), or *Zenkyōtō* in shorthand, were radical leftist organizations instrumental in organizing student activism from 1968 to the early 1970s. This period after the student protest against the ratification of U.S.–Japan Security Treaty in 1960 marks the second peak of student activism in postwar Japan, characterized by many campus closures, physical struggles with universities that often turned violent, and bloody infighting. For many who participated in the activism as university students, these events served as a shared experience which tied the generation together. This generation became known as the "*zenkyōtō* generation." Azuma's "first generation of the otaku," following the *zenkyōtō* generation by about a decade, is known to be much less political, and for the otaku of this generation the defining generational experience is watching the same anime series and participating in the fan activities.—Trans.]

20. [We have chosen to translate *monogatari*, literally "the telling of things," as "narrative." This term has been used both as a description of genre and as a theoretical concept. Though the term stems back to premodern literature and is often translated as "tale," as in *The Tale of Genji (Genji monogatari)*, we have chosen to translate the difficult term *monogatari* as "narrative" to place the text in direct dialogue with postmodern theory. But it should always be remembered that in Japanese the idea of an *ōkina monogatari* or "grand narrative" not only hearkens back to theorists like Lyotard but also further back to the premodern classics.—Trans.]

21. [This was true as of 2001, when the Japanese version of the present work was published. In 2006, Gainax announced the plan for *Rebuild of Evangelion*, a sequel to the *Evangelion* franchise, or a "new century" edition, in the form of tetralogy of feature-length anime films. The first episode was released in Japan in September 2007, and other episodes are planned to follow.—Trans.]

22. See Shiota Nobuyuki and CB's Project, eds., *Fukakutei sekai no tantei shinshi: Wārudo gaidansu* (The detective gentleman of the uncertain world: A guidance to the world) (Tokyo: Softbank Publishing, 2000), 129ff.

23. http://www.tinami.com.

24. Nanohana Koneko, *Di Gi Charat*, vol. 2 (Tokyo: Kadokawa Dengeki Bunko, 2000), 12, 19–20.

25. [Such as "*sōda-nyo*" ("yes-nyo") and "*tsukareta-nyo*" ("I'm tired-nyo"). The sound "nyo" sounds similar to the cry of a cat, like "meow" in English. —Trans.]

26. [The "nurturing simulation games" are simulation games (mostly on PC or game consoles) in which the player's goal is to "nurture" *(ikusei)* a character—anything from a race horse to a virtual creature—to the best possible form. The popular handheld digital pet "Tamagocchi" can be considered as an extension of this genre. There is a subset of this genre in which, in a cross with the "love simulation game," the player nurtures a young girl to a young lady, and hopefully his dream lover—arguably in the spirit of Shining Genji marrying a Young Murasaki in *The Tale of Genji* or Humbert Humbert's raising of Lolita in the Nabokov novel. Gainax's *Princess Maker,* the PC simulation game first released in 1991, popularized the "nurturing simulation games" featuring young girls, and "Ayanami Nurturing Project" belongs in this lineage.—Trans.]

27. [Sadamoto Yoshiyuki (1962–) is a manga artist, character designer, and animator who has worked on many famous anime, but is best known as character designer for *Neon Genesis Evangelion.*—Trans.]

28. [*Nadesico* was first created as a manga series by Mamiya Kia, "Yūgeki uchū senkan nadeshiko" (Mobile space battleship Nadesico), *Gekkan shōnen ésu* (Monthly "boys' ace") September 1996–February 1999. Only one month after the beginning of the manga serialization, it was produced as a TV anime series, directed by Satō Tatsuo ("Kidō senkan nadeshiko" [Mobile battleship Nadesico], TV Tokyo, October 1, 1996–March 25, 1997). It was also made into an anime film by the same director, released on August 8, 1998. While the manga version shares the names of the characters with the anime versions, the character data and the plot are vastly different. Both the TV series and the film credits Mamiya for "Character Original Design" *(Kyarakutā gen'an),* the extent of her involvement in the anime version, if any, and her influence on the anime version is unknown.—Trans.]

29. [Seiryōin Ryūsui (b. 1974) is an author of mystery novels. The kanji characters of his pseudonym reads "Water Stream of the Clean and Cool Temple."—Trans.]

30. [*Kozumikku* (Cosmic) (Tokyo: Kōdansha Novels, 1996); *Jōkā* (Joker) (Tokyo: Kōdansha Novels, 1997); *19 Bokkusu* (Jukebox) (Tokyo: Kōdansha Novels, 1997); *Kānibaru* (Carnival) (Tokyo: Kōdansha Novels, 1999).—Trans.]

31. [*"Taisetsu"* (literally "great story") is a pun, in contrast with the Japanese word for novel (*"shōsetsu"* [literally "small story"]), a standard literary term for narrative fiction.—Trans.]

32. Ōtsuka Eiji, *Monogatari no taisō* (Workouts of fiction) (Tokyo: Asahi Shinbunsha, 2000), 198ff.

33. [Azuma is invoking the notion of *shasei* (literally, "copying life") or vivid description of life—a key concept of realism in modern Japanese literature first proposed by the poet Masaoka Shiki (1867–1902), which profoundly influenced Japanese naturalism of the era. As Ōtsuka argues below, the notion

of realism in this period was influenced by European fiction, and therefore it was perceived as a borrowing from the West.—Trans.]

34. [Ayatsuji Yukito (b. 1960) and Norizuki Rintarō (b. 1964) are both popular writers of detective fiction, often referred to as *shin-honkakuha* (neoclassic).—Trans.]

35. On the deconstruction of "codes" in mystery in 1990s Japan, the most useful discussion can be found in Kasai Kiyoshi, *Tantei shōsetsuron II* (On detective fiction II) (Tokyo: Tokyo Sōgensha, 1998).

36. [Kyōgoku Natsuhiko (b. 1963) is a popular novelist best known for his horror and mystery novels. Mori Hiroshi (b. 1957) is an author of mystery novels. Both are prolific and their mystery worlds have many fans.—Trans.]

37. Seiryōin Ryūsui, *Kozumikku* (Cosmic) (Tokyo: Kōdansha Novels, 1996), 275.

38. Walter Benjamin, "The Work of Art in the Age of Mechanical Reproduction," in *Illuminations*, ed. Hannah Arendt, trans. Harry Zohn, 217–52 (New York: Schocken Books, 1969).

39. Baudrillard, *Symbolic Exchange and Death*, 2.

40. Ibid., 64.

41. For example, Figure 15 is a life-size figurine called "Type B" of the Second Mission Project Ko^2 sequence. It is conceived as the middle of an imaginary transformation process from the girl type (Type A) to the battle airplane type (Type C). This work is stuffed with otaku devices, such as green hair and a white bodysuit, but the most remarkable design factor is a realistic vagina inscribed in the head of the airplane.

The psychiatrist Saitō Tamaki, whom I will mention below, argues in *Sentō bishōjo no seishin bunseki* (The psychoanalysis of battling beautiful girls) (Tokyo: Ōta Shuppan, 2000) that the sexual desire of the otaku is directed to "a girl identified with a phallus," who is a "thoroughly empty existence." The "battling beautiful girl" is an image of such a girl. In other words, the girl images consumed in otaku culture basically have nothing to do with real women but are projections of the otaku's own obsession with his own phallus, i.e., a fetish object created by the projection of narcissism. The Second Mission Project Ko^2 sequence, in which a naked girl is transformed into a phallic-shaped machine, is guided by the very insight that Saitō is describing here. Here Murakami is realizing the hidden structure that equates the battling beautiful girl with the otaku's own phallus in this work and is sticking it to the otaku, in the shape of a vagina inscribed in the phallic-shaped airplane head. One can understand the attractiveness and critical edge of Murakami's works very well in the context discussed above.

42. Murakami's comment during a panel discussion by Asano Masahiko, Murakami, and myself, entitled "To Make the Invisible Visible" during the aforementioned Wonder Festival 2000. [See note 19 of chapter 1.—Trans.]

43. Sawaraki Noi's definition. See Sawaraki Noi, *Simyurēshonizumu* (Simulationism) (Tokyo: Kawade Bunko, 1994), 11.

44. Alexandre Kojève, *Introduction to the Reading of Hegel* (New York: Basic Books, 1969).

45. Ibid., 160n.

46. See Kojève, *Introduction to the Reading of Hegel*, 159n. [For the quotations of philosophical texts, the published English translation is used unless otherwise noted.—Trans.]

47. Okada, *Otakugaku nyūmon*, 121.

48. [The "squadron special effects dramas" or "super *sentai* series" are superhero TV shows for children produced by Tōhō, in which a team of human-size superheroes (usually five to seven members, each typically assigned a specific color) engages in a struggle against an empire of monsters. *Himitsu Sentai Goranger* (1975–77) was the first such show, and, as of 2007, there have been thirty-one shows in this series. In the United States, since 1993, these shows have been adapted into the very popular *Mighty Morphin Power Rangers* shows.—Trans.]

49. [The original Japanese for "idea" here is *shukō*. See chapter 1, note 17, for the notions of "an idea" as a central concept in traditional poetics of Kabuki upon which Okada is drawing here.—Trans.]

50. Kojève, *Introduction to the Reading of Hegel*, 162.

51. Slavoj Žižek, *The Sublime Object of Ideology* (London: Verso, 1989), 197–98.

52. Peter Sloterdijk, *Critique of Cynical Reason*, Theory and History of Literature 40 (Minneapolis: University of Minnesota Press, 1987), 122.

53. Ōsawa, *Denshi media ron*, 279, 286. [The original term for "the agency of the third party" is "dai sansha no shinkyū." *Shinkyū* is a legal term referring to the level of agency in the court system—"instance" as in "a court of first instance." "The agency of the third party" is the imaginary agency, some absolute Other, to which one refers when there are disagreements on laws or rules among individuals. See, for example, Ōsawa Masachi, "Komyunikēshon to kisoku" (Communication and rules) in *Imi to tashasei* (Meaning and otherness), 3–97 (Tokyo: Keisō shobō, 1994), esp. 78–95.—Trans.]

54. [Ōsawa, *Kyokō no jidai no hate*; Ōsawa Masachi, *Sengo no shisō kūkan* (Postwar intellectual space) (Tokyo: Chikuma shinsho, 1998).—Trans.]

55. Ōsawa, *Sengo no shisō kūkan*, 228; Ōsawa, *Kyokō no jidai no hate*, 40.

56. [See Louis Althusser, "Ideology and Ideological State Apparatuses (Notes towards an Investigation)," trans. Ben Brewster, in *Lenin and Philosophy and Other Essays* (New York: Monthly Review Press, 1971).—Trans.]

57. For a quick overview of the history of "girl games," see Pasokon Bishōjo Gēmu Kenkyūkai, ed., *Pasokon bishōjo gēmu rekishi taizen* (A complete history of PC 'beautiful girls games') (Tokyo: Bunkasha, 2000).

58. The freeware I used here is Susie32 (ver. 0.45a), with plug-ins Leaf PAK AX ver. 0.27 and Leaf CG to DIB ver. 0.27.

59. To be exact, the terms Kojève uses are "human desire" and "animal desire"; however, since his distinction is too intricate for our purposes, I rephrased them with the technical terminology of Lacanian psychoanalysis. In the Lacanian school, "desire" *(désir)* refers to human desire only, and for what Kojève called "animal desire," the term "needs" *(besoin)* is assigned. [See Jacques Lacan, "The Signification of the Phallus," in *Écrits,* trans. Bruce Fink, 575–85 (New York: Norton, 2006).—Trans.]

60. Kojève, *Introduction to the Reading of Hegel,* 159.

61. See, for example, Saitō Tamaki, *Sentō bishōjo no seishin bunseki,* 53.

62. ["Yaoi" is a genre of sexually explicit stories (manga or novels) or fan art featuring male–male sex written and consumed predominantly by women. Often it takes the form of a "derivative work" (discussed in this book), with characters borrowed from famous manga/anime series, and is published in fanzines and sold/shared over the Internet and at the Comiket. The vast majority of the creators and consumers of yaoi are heterosexual women, prompting speculations and theories about the underlying desires for this practice. See also Sharon Kinsella, *Adult Manga: Culture and Power in Contemporary Japanese Society* (London: Routledge, 2000).—Trans.]

63. Nonetheless, I wish to reserve judgment on the female otaku, whose consumption centers on the yaoi genre. Within my limited experience with them, the creative motive and the consumption behavior of the female otaku who love the yaoi genre is far more human than the consumers of girl games, who have been completely animalized, and the behavior of these female otaku seems intimately related to the question of sexuality. As I mentioned in note 14 in chapter 1, this book focuses more on the male otaku than the female otaku, and I have avoided mentioning this significant aspect of otaku culture. Meanwhile, just by observing the business trends in this genre, even the female otaku are beginning to be animalized and database-ized, among the younger generations. Unfortunately I have not done enough research and do not understand the exact circumstances in this area.

64. [*Kogal* refers to a high-school-girl fashion style popular in the mid-1990s and characterized by brown-dyed hair and overly large socks ("loose socks"). The media at that time covered their lifestyles extensively, portraying them as promiscuous girls willing to engage in "compensated dating" (See note 34 in chapter 1), but it is questionable how much of the media hype was based in reality.—Trans.]

65. Miyadai Shinji, *Seifuku shōjo tachi no sentaku* (The choice of the school uniform girls) (Tokyo: Kōdansha, 1994).

66. [*Shinjinrui* (new Homo sapiens) was the term popularized by the journalist Chikushi Tetsuya in the mid-1980s, referring to young creators and

professionals who are doing trailblazing works in their respective fields in a manner unconstrained by tradition. The meaning of the term later expanded to refer to the whole generation of young people who share the same sensibility. The image of *shinjinrui* is often linked to the rise of otaku culture, as Okada's use of the term "new type" suggests (see note 8 of chapter 1), and also the New Academism movements.—Trans.]

67. Miyadai, *Seifuku shōjo tachi no sentaku*, 248, 267.

68. Miyadai Shinji, *Owari naki nichijō o ikiro* (Live the endless everyday) (Tokyo: Chikuma bunko, 1998), 168.

69. [Azuma is referring to the problems of "futōkō" (school refusal) and "hikikomori" (acute social withdrawal), both of which have been widely recognized as social problems among youth in the 1990s. "School refusal" is the phenomenon in which students are unwilling to attend schools for reasons that vary from bullying to poor academic performance. *Hikikomori* is the phenomenon in which young adults (many of them male) withdraw themselves in their own rooms, are unable to engage in any type of social activities including school and work. The national television network, NHK, estimates that there are between half a million to a million people who would fall in this category. (See the *hikikomori* support site at NHK: http://www.nhk.or.jp/fnet/hikikomori/qa/index.html.) Experts cite psychiatric factors such as pervasive developmental disorders and social factors such as the lack of communication skills as possible causes. These phenomena have received much media attention in the 1990s and provoked social commentaries and discussions. Miyadai was one of the most influential critics in such discussions.—Trans.]

3. Hyperflatness and Multiple Personality

1. *Nikkei BP dejitaru daijiten* (Nikkei BP digital encyclopedia), 3rd ed. (Tokyo: Nikkei BP Sha, 2000), 430.

2. To be exact, there are ways to avoid this problem, by using the style sheets or using the JavaScript to detect which browser the user is using, but here I am only discussing the basic features. In any case, even the World Wide Web Consortium strongly recommends separating the markup for the logical structure of contents from the markup for the presentation effects. See Web Content Accessibility Guidelines 1.0 (http://www.w3.org/TR/WCAG/).

3. Needless to say, these few tags and scripts cannot exhaust all of the meanings and contents of a Web page. The syntax of HTML, and moreover the computer culture that gave rise to it, fundamentally has the passion to turn the formerly "invisible" semantic realm into the "visible," encoded, and logical. Computer science or information theory, from the beginning, was and is a science that holds as its ideal to make everything visible and operable. In the context of intellectual history, this tendency has been inherited from the logical positivism of the early twentieth century. As the Internet has become

more popular and the computer more multimedia, such intellectual tendencies might seem more vague, but the underlying trends remain unchanged.

4. [The word Azuma uses here, *chōheimenteki*, is influenced by "superflat," the concept that Murakami Takashi used to characterize the artistic movement centered on his own works. Nonetheless, *chōheimenteki* or "hyperflatness" is a narrow concept that describes the characteristics of the postmodern semiotic world, and therefore it is quite different from Murakami's concept. Murakami's "superflat" is a sensuous term, incorporating not only the visual characteristics of his works but also the characteristics of social structure and communications. "Chō-heimenteki" is a term Azuma coined from *chō-* (ultra-, hyper-, or super-) and *heimenteki* (flat-like), distinguishing his term more clearly from Murakami's "superflat" than what is rendered here in English.—Trans.]

5. [The original Japanese for the term "hypervisual" is *kashiteki,* another term Azuma coined from *ka-* (excessive), *shi-teki* (visual).—Trans.]

6. In the past I used the term "postal anxiety" to describe the same situation. See Azuma, *Yūbin teki fuantachi* (Postal anxieties) (Tokyo: Asahi Shinbunsha, 1999).

7. [In Japan, visual novels have been a major genre of PC adventure games for many years. In a visual novel the player plays the protagonist, and makes choices on his or her actions, much like the "choose your own adventure" books in the United States. The player follows multiple story lines and arrives at one of the many endings. It is often accompanied with the graphics.—Trans.]

8. See chapter 3 of Ian Hacking, *Rewriting the Soul: Multiple Personality and the Science of Memory* (Princeton, N.J.: Princeton University Press, 1995). [See also Elaine Showalter, *Hystories* (New York: Columbia University Press, 1998).—Trans.]

9. Daniel Keyes, *The Minds of Billy Milligan* (New York: Random House, 1995), 33.

10. Ibid., 186

11. A. M. Ludwig et al., "The Objective Study of a Multiple Personality: Or, Are Four Heads Better Than One?" *Archives of General Psychiatry* 26: 298–310. For details of the issue of memory in multiple personality, see chapter 6 of Frank W. Putnam, *Dissociation in Children and Adolescents: A Developmental Perspective* (New York: Guilford Press, 1997).

Index

Hiroki Azuma is codirector of the Academy of Humanities in the Center for the Study of World Civilizations at the Tokyo Institute of Technology. A leading cultural critic in Japan, he is the author of seven books, including *Ontological, Postal,* which won the 2000 Suntory Literary Prize.

Jonathan E. Abel is assistant professor of comparative literature at The Pennsylvania State University.

Shion Kono is assistant professor of literature at Sophia University, Tokyo, Japan.